FROM THE INSIDE **OUT**

Leading Where it Matters Most

The How-to Guide

to Leading Nonprofits for Impact

TOM OKARMA

Copyright © 2019 Tom Okarma
All rights reserved.
ISBN: 9781081357122

FROM THE INSIDE OUT

For Julie & Jenny

May you always keep your servant's hearts, continue helping others, and restoring hope to those in need.

CONTENTS

PART 1: Leading Yourself

1	The Good, The Bad, & The Unknown	Pg 7
2	Do You Have What it Takes to Be Great?	Pg 15
3	You and Only You	Pg 33

PART 2: Leading The Organization

4	Leadership: The Best of The Best	Pg 65
5	Leading Your Team	Pg 71
6	Leading Your *Other* Team	Pg 81

PART 3: Leading The Board

7	Your Board's Role in the Organization	Pg 97
8	The Makings of A Great Board Director	Pg 103
9	From Great Players to an Incredible *Team*	Pg 113
10	What a Great Board *Does*	Pg 151
11	Houston, We Have a Problem	Pg 163

PART 4: Leading Change

12	Getting Ready for Change	Pg 177
13	Planning for Change	Pg 187
14	Planning for Potholes & Detours	Pg 201
15	Making it All Work	Pg 211
16	The End is Never Really Near	Pg 219

	Epilogue: What to Do When You're Stuck	Pg 223
	About the Author	Pg 227

INTRODUCTION

From The Inside Out

Why are there so many "great" leadership books and yet so few great leaders?

I've asked myself this many times… Spend a minute wandering down the business aisle at your local bookstore — you know, that place you go for coffee and to read the magazines for free — or take just a few seconds to browse *Leadership* on Amazon and you'll be overwhelmed with how many books claim to hold all the answers to your leadership challenges.

And if you're anything like me (and I secretly hope you are, since you're holding my book) chances are you even own several of them — maybe even lots of them.

We've been studying behavior, productivity, efficiency, and leadership since one cave man surfaced, figured out he could get the others to hunt bear for him, and threatened to beat them with his club if they didn't do it, and do it fast.

A perfect solution at first, until the other cave men quickly tired of his tyrant behavior and refused to give him any of the food…

Throwing their clubs in the air they set fire to his cave before he could retaliate, and quickly grunted their votes for a new leader. Under new leadership their hunting became more efficient, leaving more time for innovation, and soon the wheel was born.

Okay... so maybe that's not exactly how it went down, but I don't think I'm off by much....

Everyone hates a dictator, but people look up to, respect, and often even love a *good* leader. Each of us — even if we are leading others — look to someone else for leadership in some area. When we look to that person, we want to see all the things we want to become.

If I asked you to name three bad leaders you've encountered, I bet it would take you about three-seconds. But if I asked you to name three good leaders you've encountered you might need a bit more time.

Leadership is hard. Good leadership is even harder. Great leadership can seem nearly impossible. But it is the great leaders that are remembered. They are the ones that bring about change. They are the ones that have significant impact.

I think we can all agree (at least all of us reading this book) that leadership — *good leadership* — is critical. And perhaps I'm a bit biased, but I believe good *nonprofit* leadership is even more critical.

You are the leaders bringing change to the world. You are the ones compelled to make a difference. You are the ones leading with heart, driven to achieve your mission and leave the world a better place than when you found it.

I've led in both the for-profit and nonprofit worlds, and I can say hands down — nonprofit leaders have it harder. Juggling the normal demands placed on a for-profit leader (team management and moving the organization forward) with the additional demands of a nonprofit — keeping donors happy, satisfying the board, managing a potential army of volunteers — all while keeping a smile on your face and being a perfect face of the organization to anyone and everyone you bump into. Oh, and don't forget saving the world — you better make that happen too… It's… exhausting.

That's why I wrote this book. Nonprofit leaders need something unique. The typical leadership book just doesn't cut it. You need something more — a leadership book that hits on *each* part of the overall challenge that is leading a nonprofit.

Since you picked up this book (and made it this far — *thank you*!) I bet you're looking for a new perspective. Perhaps some new ideas or methods you can try to make things happen.

You want your team to do more on their own, your board to be better, your plan for progress to actually work. Let's face it. You want change. You want your organization to make a bigger impact, and you know at the core of that is you. If you could just somehow find a way to be the leader you were born to be, you know you can make it happen. I'm here to tell you you're right. You *can* make change happen, even if it's failed before. You *can* get your nonprofit to the next level. You *can* make a bigger impact. And this book will tell you how to get there.

Great leadership begins from the inside out. It starts with you. You will never lead your organization or board to change if you haven't first mastered the art of leading yourself. But succeed there and you will be unstoppable.

This book is broken into four parts, each designed to build on each other. But just in case you're human and don't want to wait until you're half way through to get to the parts you want most, I'll give you a shortcut.

Work through Part 1 first, then skip to the section that lines up best with your most urgent challenge. This will help you get the most value out of the book fastest. Once you've gained insight, I invite you to go back to the other sections. You might be pleasantly surprised at what you learn and how your leadership in other areas will improve.

This is not a read-in-one-sitting kind of book. Many of the chapters contain questions at the end for you to evaluate your organization and leadership. They will require you to pause and reflect. If you want to get as much as possible from the book, you'll want to take a few minutes to answer each of the questions as honestly as you can. If you take the time to do the work, I promise you it will pay off in the end.

And now let's begin your journey *From the Inside Out*.

PART 1:

LEADING YOURSELF

FROM THE INSIDE OUT

CHAPTER 1

The Good, The Bad, & The Unknown
Leading Yourself First

Before you can successfully lead others, you must first know how to lead yourself.

Each day you're pulled in a hundred directions at once. Called upon to balance a variety of important factors—people, problems, budgets, priorities, strategies, etc.

To make it all work you have to have *self-confidence* and an *unwavering commitment to the agency's mission*. This can only be done well when you understand your own strengths, weaknesses, preferences, style, competencies, and values. You must know your own professional make up — strengths *and* weaknesses.

Unless you are comfortable in your own skin and firmly anchored in your values, you might waiver when making decisions, treat everything as relative, and be seen by others as inconsistent. Such a leader will have trouble building or leading an effective team or successful organization.

FROM THE INSIDE OUT

Featured in Harvard Business Review article *Managing Oneself,* Peter Drucker said:

"To do things well, you'll need to cultivate a deep understanding of yourself, and only when you operate from strengths can you achieve true excellence."

But he goes on to warn us about relying on skills and strengths alone in our pursuit of leadership.

"What one does well—even very well and successfully—may not fit with one's value system."

Leading only from one's strengths and skill, without having a set of values to guide your judgement and leadership, can lead to ethical and moral problems.

Think of the infamous hacker. Threatening millions of systems and users each day. They certainly possess — and perhaps even manage — from certain skills, but they are void of the values it takes to be a true leader. It takes skills, strengths *and* values to be a successful and respected leader.

Drucker goes on in the article to emphasize the importance of a *self-inventory* and raises the following self-management questions:

- What are your strengths?
- How do you perform?
- How do you learn?
- What are your values?
- Where do you belong?
- What should you contribute?

Expanding on Drucker's questions, I believe leaders should review themselves using these questions, bearing in mind the need to be brutally honest. I invite you to take a moment and answer these questions. If you're unsure of the answers — and you definitely won't be alone — you may find yourself struggling to lead from a place of confidence.

- What are my values? What is most important?
- How do I live these values out?
- What do they look like each day?
- What are the skills that I do well?
- What do I do better than anyone else?
- What are my strengths and weaknesses?

**Faking it never works for true leaders.
Neither does intimidation or indecisiveness.**

Fake it till you make it. We've all heard it. But does it actually work? When a leader lacks self-confidence, clarity in their own values, or is unsure of the agency's future direction, everyone around will see it… and it's not pretty. If people believe you're in over your head, you'll have a hard time recovering. In order to lead well, a leader must both know themselves and regularly practice effective leadership techniques.

By knowing yourself, you need an understanding of which skills you are gifted with and which ones you may not be. It's important to remember, *each of us* have a unique set of talents and gifts. But it's equally important to realize that *none of us* has been given an endless supply of talents and gifts. Now, don't get me wrong. I truly see great nonprofit leaders as superheroes in their own right, but it takes time and effort — *lots of it* — to get to that point. And don't forget... even Batman had Robin.

It can take a little bit of brutal honesty to admit potential areas of weakness, but it can also be freeing as now you know what skills gaps need to be filled by others. Having Robin didn't make Batman weaker, it made him stronger. It bears repeating. Robin made Batman stronger. Capable of doing more, focusing on his unique strengths, and working together as a team to save the world.

Leaders become great when they lead from their strengths, face their weaknesses head on, and fill their team with people who are gifted in those areas the leader may not be.

It's likely you already know which skills and competencies you do really well, and which ones you can perform reasonably well. You may already have some understanding of which areas give you trouble. To lead a successful organization, you need to surround yourself with people who are better skilled in your weaker areas and rely on their expertise. I know it can be tough, but I've been there too...

In my previous days of leading a 300+ person organization, the leadership team and I would spend a decent amount of time reviewing financials. While we understood the basics, we weren't analyzing our financial reports at a level we should — to gain true insight. I knew we needed something more. Fortunately, we found an outstanding number cruncher who understood the finances inside and out. He was skilled at not only translating those numbers into plain English, but effectively communicating what the reports were actually telling us.

Knowing yourself, and understanding your strengths, skills, and values, will make you a better leader. Remember, few if any leaders are gifted with every skill needed to succeed. Identifying, understanding, and complementing your weaknesses with a strong and diverse team, will help setup both you and the organization for success.

Since we all tend to have a biased view of our own skills, it can helpful to seek impartial, outside help. There are a wide variety of tools available — in the way of behavioral assessments, personality assessments and leadership evaluations. I've taken many of them at different times during my career and found them to be spot on. I came to better understand what skills I was proficient in performing and which I needed to develop.

I was once evaluated with an assessment known as the 360 Review. While a bit daunting at first, it's a very powerful tool. It assessed my performance and leadership skills by asking my boss, my team, and peers a series of confidential questions. It looks at a leader from all sides to give you a full picture. From the review I discovered four unique challenges that were holding me back.

1. My reviewers combined to remind me that as CEO, I owned our mission and vision and needed to send clear, consistent, and frequent messages to our employees. I needed to reinforce our top 2-3 priorities and why they were so critical. This would help provide clarity and identify any disconnect between our mission and what we were actually doing. To get better in this area I began to invest a lot of my time in staff meetings reviewing what we were trying to accomplish, why we felt it was the best course of action for us and evaluate our progress.

2. I also learned at times I was inadvertently overshadowing some of my staff when we had guests in the building. I tried to carefully manage my presence as the CEO so they could shine in front to the others. However, they also felt I should increase my direct involvement with these partners and guests, being careful to not disrupt their roles.

3. The responders said I should be clearer in mission and vision regarding what risks we would be willing to take and where to draw a boundary line in the sand. Yet, they also said I should ensure we were moving at the speed of the marketplace. They wanted me to ensure things got done and decisions were made in a timely fashion.

4. Finally, they felt we needed to celebrate our successes more and that I needed to be a big part of that effort. I can be pretty task oriented, tending to focus on getting things done and can easily forget that we need to take time to celebrate and thank everyone for their efforts. We soon implemented the occasional office pizza lunches, Friday afternoon ice cream socials, and other activities designed to celebrate our accomplishments as a team and company.

I cannot overstate how helpful tools like the 360 Review and other assessments can be, to sharpen your leadership. You will come to know yourself better, how your leadership is perceived by others, and what steps you need to take to be better.

To start or continue your self-discovery journey -- as well as gain some immediate feedback and insight -- I invite you to take the Leadership Styles Test on my website.

Visit www.TomOkarma.com/Learn

CHAPTER 2

Do You Have What It Takes to Be Great?
The 11 Characteristics of Effective Self-Leadership

Nearly all men can stand adversity, but if you want to test a man's character, give him power. – President Abraham Lincoln

Do you know what makes you tick? Do you know what works for you and what doesn't? Do you know what motivates you and what tends to make you stuck? Do you know your strengths and weaknesses, where you excel and where you have challenges? Have you mastered the art of effective *Self Leadership*?

In my decades of experience working with leaders there are a few characteristics that I have found to set a truly great leader apart from the rest and predict their likelihood of success.

I call these the 11 Characteristics of Great Self Leadership. Do you see them in your own leadership? As you learn more about each of the 11 traits, I invite you to evaluate yourself after each characteristic.

1. INTEGRITY
(Trust, Honesty, Ethical Behavior)

You set the tone for others on what is acceptable and non-acceptable behavior by how you conduct yourself. A leader has nothing if they do not have the trust of their team. Most people rely on a leader to model what trust, integrity, and ethical behavior look like in an agency and expect them to consistently act that way — even (especially) during tough times. It may be tempting to rationalize making a few *less-then-ideal* choices during a crisis, but when a leader takes a situational ethics approach to decision-making, he/she cannot undo it later. Your team will notice and always remember. This can weaken your leadership and ability to positively influence in the future.

Remember, social media has ushered in an era of transparency. Your actions can speak volumes -- even if you say nothing.

Self-Evaluation
Do you lead with Integrity?

Does your team trust you? Do you model ethical behavior? What would you give yourself?

Integrity > 1 2 3 4 5 6 7 8 9 10

Think about a time recently where you had a tough opportunity. How did you handle it? Did you lead with integrity or take the easier road?

2. MORAL COURAGE

The old saying goes…"What's right is right and what's wrong is wrong" but it's not always that simple. There are times where you may be faced with a gray area. A leader should show courage when faced with challenging situations by making the hard, but right calls. Shrinking away from a tough call or delegating it to someone else undermines a leader and damages their ability to lead in the future. It takes courage to say and do the right thing yet that is what we leaders are supposed to do.

In our hearts, we often know the difference between right and wrong, but sometimes it can be a still quiet voice. If you're not immediately sure what the right or wrong answer is, allow yourself a little quiet time. If that little voice in your head is questioning your decision, you know what you need to do. Remember, others are always watching how you perform and how you handle your toughest challenges.

In my time as a leader I've had to terminate or reassign people from time to time. In two cases, I was asked what took me so long? The honest truth is I didn't want to believe what I had heard from others around the office about these two people. I suspect a few team members thought I was playing favorites, but I wasn't. I wanted to believe the best of all of my people. But as a leader it's your job to make the tough calls. I suspect my delay in taking action lost me some credibility for a period of time.

Self-Evaluation
Do you lead with Moral Courage?

Do you make the tough (right) decisions when needed?
What would you give yourself?

Courage > 1 2 3 4 5 6 7 8 9 10

Think about a time recently where you had an opportunity to act with Moral Courage. How did you handle it?

_____

3. TRANSPARENCY

It's important to be as open and forthcoming as possible with others — especially your board and your team. The more you share with them, the fewer questions they will have and the better they can fulfill their roles. If you fail to provide relevant, important information, most people will try to fill-in the gaps with what they already know, or worse, what they suspect. There is no limit to what a damaging dose of "palace intrigue" can do to an otherwise well-run agency.

Transparency is one personal characteristic your team needs to see in you before they will trust you. My experience is that teams want to trust their leader and are willing to go to great lengths for them — assuming they have a reasonable grasp of what is going on.

Self-Evaluation
Do you lead with Transparency?

Do you provide clear information to your team?
What would you give yourself?

Transparency > 1 2 3 4 5 6 7 8 9 10

Think about a time recently where you had an opportunity to act with Transparency.
How did you handle it?

---

4. VALUES-DRIVEN

Does your organization have values? Simple words that help define how you will conduct yourself as an agency? Values like teamwork, trust, integrity, accountability, etc.?

Values set the tone for the organization and are often responsible for creating the culture and dictating how people treat each other and customers. A critical piece of any new employee or volunteer orientation program is the explanation and review of the agency's values. But explaining them isn't enough. Keep in mind, these new additions will pay close attention and watch to see if anyone actually follows them.

If agency values are not observed and acted out by everyone — *especially you as the leader* — it will be seen that you have no values. This can lead to relativism and chaos. Everyone makes up their own definition of the values. You should strive to be a 24x7 living example of what your values look like when they are followed. Everyone will be watching you.

This also applies when you learn someone else has violated a value. All eyes will be on you watching to see how you handle the situation, and if you apply the values (and any consequences) consistently from person to person.

Self-Evaluation
Do you lead by example with Values?

Do you take time to explain values? Do you pay attention to situations where the values are used or forgotten? Do you reward positive situations and provide consequences for negative situations?
What would you give yourself?

Values > 1 2 3 4 5 6 7 8 9 10

Think about a time recently where you had an opportunity to teach or enforce Values.
How did you handle it?

_____

5. RESPECT

Everyone you encounter—clients, your team, volunteers, board members, donors, key partners, etc. — deserves to be treated fairly. You should demonstrate courtesy and respect even when someone makes an inexcusable, colossal error or bad decision. Others will be watching how you handle yourself and irreparable damage can be done to your internal relationships if you use your position/power incorrectly.

It's easy to be respectful when things are going well. It can be far more challenging to act with respect when a team member has made a mistake, or a client is upset with you. Try to put yourself in their shoes and act with the courtesy you would want to be shown in the same situation.

Self-Evaluation
Do you lead with Respect?

Do you treat others (all others) fairly and with professionalism?
What would you give yourself?

Respect > 1 2 3 4 5 6 7 8 9 10

Think about a time recently where you had an opportunity to act with Respect.
How did you handle it?

6. HUMILITY

It takes your entire team to deliver on your mission and serve your clients. You can't do it alone. When a leader is first to take the credit and last to take the blame, they alienate their team and create a wall between each other. Your team will respond infinitely better if you generously share all credit with them. In fact, look for ways to feature them to the rest of your team, outsiders, the board, or even the community.

Several times as a leader I've tried to give team members a chance to speak before the board whenever possible. They usually knew their report better than I, which enabled them to shine, develop their skills, and interact with the board in a meaningful way.

I remember the first leadership team meeting I chaired when I took over a for-profit company. I knew right away my first responsibility was to keep my ego in check and do all I could to help those around me, succeed in their roles. That was the only way the organization (and I) would succeed.

Self-Evaluation
Do you lead with Humility?

Are you quick to provide credit and slow to give blame? What would you give yourself?
What would you give yourself?

Humility > 1 2 3 4 5 6 7 8 9 10

> Think about a time recently where you had an opportunity to act with Humility.
> How did you handle it?

---

7. ENCOURAGEMENT & POSITIVITY

Everyone needs encouragement. Not everyone needs it in the same way. For some people a quick word in passing about the success of a project will be enough. Others may need an occasional uplifting message from you. Still a few others — who may take their responsibilities, successes, and failures to heart — may need a bit more.

We all have bad days. But as the leader we can't bring those bad days (or bad attitudes) into the office. Others will get nervous and distracted if they see us down or discouraged. Leaders need to be sensitive to their team members because they could be under tremendous outside pressures (family, financial, personal) that could be adding to their work pressure. An uplifting word of encouragement, thanks, or appreciation from you is powerful and can be just what someone needs to get through the day.

Not great with encouragement? Many leaders struggle with this. Once of the best ways you can help encourage your team is to engage with them periodically on their work. Ask how they are doing.

Ask about a problem they are dealing with. Ask how they think the problem could be resolved. Sometimes encouragement can come in the form of you agreeing with their approach to solving a problem.

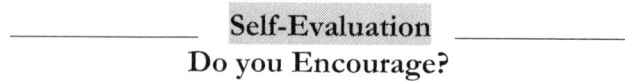

Do you Encourage?

Do you provide affirmation for your team when they are struggling? What would you give yourself?

Encouragement > 1 2 3 4 5 6 7 8 9 10

Think about a time recently where you had an opportunity to Encourage. How did you handle it?

_____

8. COLLABORATION

I once took over an organization that had several separate departments that rarely spoke to each other. Picture a row of silos, all aligned next to each other, but not touching. This was the condition of the company. No one thought much about the other units, few even knew what other units did, they rarely worked on projects together, and, in a few occasions, they actually worked against each other's best interests.

You will get the very best results when you create task forces or teams with members from different departments and then encourage them to find ways to work together on their common assignment.

A great way to encourage collaboration within your team is through shadowing. Have a team member from one department or area spend a few hours (or even a whole day) shadowing someone from another area. Let them experience the unique challenges facing that department. Help them see things from a new perspective. Encourage them to ask questions and see how one universal company challenge might be viewed differently from each department.

You can also encourage collaboration by uniting everyone around a common shared mission, vision, or goal. Bring all of the teams together and clearly communicate what a specific project or initiative should look like when it has been successfully completed. Take time to share what role each department or team will play in completing the project. Give each team an opportunity to ask questions and understand how their decisions and/or actions can affect the others.

Self-Evaluation
Do you lead with Collaboration?

Do you encourage your team to work together to solve problems? Do you attempt to share multiple perspectives? What would you give yourself?

Collaboration > 1 2 3 4 5 6 7 8 9 10

> Think about a time recently where you had an opportunity to encourage Collaboration. How did you handle it?

---

9. EMPOWERMENT

People today are well educated, well trained, and want to learn even more. In fact, one of the top reasons people leave organizations is lack of opportunity for advancement and/or lack of personal development.

The best way to provide them with learning and personal growth opportunities is to give them new assignments and experiences that may be just at the edge of their current skill set. Give them a chance to stretch and grow by asking them to work on something interesting and challenging. One of your most important roles as the leader, is developing more leaders.

Make it a priority to touch base with your team members on a regular basis and find out about their interests. What other areas of the organization are they interested in learning about? What skills would they like to develop? Maybe you have someone in client services that would like to learn about development and fundraising. Showing interest in where your team members want to be in the future will communicate volumes about how you see them.

Everyone wants to go beyond where they currently are. It's your job as a leader to help learn where your people want to go and see what you can do to help them on that path.

Self-Evaluation
Do you Empower your team?

Do you learn about their interests? Do you find ways to teach new skills? What would you give yourself?

Empowerment > 1 2 3 4 5 6 7 8 9 10

Think about a time recently where you had an opportunity to Empower your team.
How did you handle it?

---

10. ADAPTABILITY

Every agency needs a plan. Yet we all know that work (and life) generally don't go according to plan. As leaders it is our job to be able to quickly and effectively adapt to change and encourage others to adapt to the situation on the ground as it presents itself. Many internal and external — *controllable and uncontrollable things* — happen along the way. A successful leader has to be able to adapt, change strategy, and be flexible.

Sometimes the best way to teach your team to be adaptable is to help them see certain situations or challenges as detours — leading temporarily away from the plan for a short time, in order to deal with a one-off challenge, etc. — and not a significant change to the overall course of the plan.

It's also important to make sure your team understands why the change is happening, and why adapting is important. By helping them see why the current track you were on may not work anymore (in light of a recent development or information) you can make the transition easier.

Self-Evaluation
Do you lead with Adaptability?

Do you have a positive attitude about change? Do you encourage your team to be flexible when things don't go as planned? What would you give yourself?

Adaptability > 1   2   3   4   5   6   7   8   9   10

Think about a time recently where you had an opportunity to lead with Adaptability.
How did you handle it?

11. PROFESSIONAL DEVELOPMENT

Your world changes very quickly with new information, new ways of doing things, new technology, and new methods of thinking popping up daily. Client needs, donor concerns, team development, leadership principles, governmental activity, technology — everything changes at warp speed — and sometimes with unanticipated impact. You know you should stay current on these topics, and you try, but sometimes it can feel like taking a drink from a fire hose.

One way to help deal with these challenges is by scheduling personal time each week (or two) to read, research, and reflect. Try to stay current on emerging industry trends and new leadership thinking and ideas.

Continuing to invest in your own knowledge, skills, and professional development not only makes you a better leader and helps increase your agency's impact, but it can also help set the tone for your culture. Showing your team that you encourage learning and growth will push them to learn too.

Sadly, training and personal development investments (time and dollars) are usually the first to get dropped from an over-booked schedule or planned expenses when things get busy or revenue becomes tight. A leader has to be committed and intentional about personal development in order to remain adequately informed.

You can do this in a few ways, either alone or with others. I suggest you partner with others to learn and grow by joining a Mastermind Group or hiring a leadership coach to help you work through your challenges. Find online communities or groups of leaders in your industry. Often, they can share insight about key changes that can save you time weeding through too much information.

Self-Evaluation
Do you make Professional Development a priority?

Do you try to stay on top of industry trends?
Are you reading something daily in your field?
Are you continually learning new things?
What would you give yourself?

Profess. Development > 1 2 3 4 5 6 7 8 9 10

Think about a time recently where you had an opportunity to invest in your Professional Development. How did you handle it?

Effective Self Leadership is critical if you want to successfully lead your team and organization. Ever heard the saying "Do as I Say, Not as I Do?" That's a bad leader. As leaders we need to set an example for our teams to follow. If we expect them to embody characteristics such as Integrity, Honesty, Adaptability, etc. we need to first show what these characteristics look like in our own role.

If you want your team to respect you, follow you, and be inspired by you as a leader you must hold yourself to a higher level. Your team will endeavor to hold themselves to the same standards.

Self-Evaluation – In Review

So how did you do? Add up your total score to gain insight into your own leadership.

- Integrity _____
- Moral Courage _____
- Transparency _____
- Values _____
- Respect _____
- Humility _____
- Encouragement _____
- Collaboration _____
- Empowerment _____
- Adaptability _____
- Professional Development _____

Your Results (Total Score) _____

Range 11-35: Danger Zone

Chances are you're really struggling to lead your team. But there is always hope if you're willing to work on developing your leadership. One-on-one coaching can help you succeed in your toughest challenges right now.

Range 36-60: Challenging

You are likely having a tough time making decisions, getting the most out of your team, and leading with influence. Many first-time leaders can fall in this category. With the right tools and support you can quickly accelerate your leadership abilities.

Range 61-95: Average

Most leaders will fall in this category. You likely excel in some areas but struggle in others. You could benefit from some one-on-one coaching to learn more about your strengths and offset your weaknesses.

Range 96-110: Leadership Excellence

Few leaders fall in this range. Those that do are generally very experienced in their roles and have invested a significant amount of time and resources in developing their leadership. But even the best leaders can continue to grow and develop.

CHAPTER 3

You and Only You
A Leader's Non-Delegable Areas of Responsibility

If you want your organization to have a bigger impact, you can't do it all yourself.

As leaders, we are often pulled in many directions each day. Donors, strategic partners, board members, community leaders, your staff, volunteers, and likely others all request a few minutes of your time and attention. Everyone has questions or thoughts they want to run by you to your opinion. On the one hand, this makes a leader feel valuable — when the questions are actually critical. But if you find yourself in a situation making all the decisions, you're probably headed towards burnout, frustrated with an endless slew of interruptions.

It can be challenging to decide where to invest your limited time. Some requests may be valid, but much of the time, those pending issues can just as well be handled by others. There's a big difference between those few things that really *need* your input, opinion, or sign off, and those where your team has simply grown accustomed to getting your stamp of approval.

So, how do you manage these frequent and interruptive requests for your time and attention in a way that allows you to focus on your top priorities, yet remain available for those things that truly need your input? How do you manage through these well intended but disruptive demands for your attention?

Many new leaders, and even some with experience, often try to accommodate each request from their team — at least at first. For a while, they make it work. After all, you're fulfilling the mission of the organization, so how could you even consider declining a meeting with a supporter or other key figure?

But eventually, they come to realize, maintaining the pace, energy, and time commitment to make everyone else happy, just isn't sustainable. At the end of the day, you're exhausted. You've put in a full day, but somehow accomplished very little and instead helped everyone else do their work. This doesn't last long before burnout begins to build. Let it get bad enough and you might actually start to resent your team.

So, what causes this and what can you do to fix it?

There are actually four challenges that surface, when a leader attempts to cater to everyone else first. To gain insight into your own leadership I invite you to pause for a moment after each of these challenges to think through your own situation.

1. You run out of time, or energy, or both.

You just can't be everywhere and do everything. There are only so many hours in the day, and you only have so much *productive* energy. Endless coffee might keep you awake, but it doesn't keep you at the top of your game. Something has to give. *Do you feel like you never have enough time to get it all done?*

2. Burnout is real and can often creep up on you.

Overextending yourself eventually leads to a decrease in the quality of your own work. Important projects suffer, key tasks get forgotten, and you might even end up "phoning it in" just to get things checked off your never-ending list. Over time you lose interest in your work, end up frustrated with your team, and key relationships begin to suffer. *Do you feel frustrated or disengaged on a regular basis?*

3. There is never time for things that matter most.

While you are busy helping others do their jobs, the key work that only you the leader can do, goes unattended. There is a reason you're the leader. You are in this role for the most important job — moving the agency forward and making a difference in lives of those you serve. There are things only you as a leader can do. If you spend all your time helping others, these critical things will fall by the wayside and the organization will fail to move forward. *Do you feel like your agency is never really making progress?*

4. You are missing out on a golden opportunity to coach and develop your team.

Once they figure out that you'll solve all their problems for them, they become dependent on your rescuing them at every turn. They will soon bring every challenge and concern to you, stop thinking on their own, and just wait for you to tell them what to do. They will become task masters, rather than strategic thinkers and problem solvers. This will lead to even more things dumped on your plate. *Do you feel like your team should be doing more on their own?*

I see it every day. Too many leaders are working below their potential, their agencies suffering because they take on too many things — much of which others should do.

Some leaders dread delegating work to others for fear it may not be done correctly. Some may struggle with communicating enough (or the right) information to their team members to get a job done. Some may not have empowered their team enough to make decisions on their own. In a few cases, leaders just like to be in control of everything, including tasks they should rightly delegate to others.

But no matter the reasons, these leaders become overwhelmed, feeling as if they are always playing catch-up, while some of their own work goes undone or suffers in quality. In their hearts, they know they aren't performing at the highest level. They may feel terrible about it, and even beat themselves up for failing to deliver. Others will simply keep trying harder, digging themselves further and further into a hole.

Please note, I'm not saying leaders shouldn't ever help others when they run into problems or have important questions — far from it. Coaching and developing others is an important part of being an effective leader. But this practice creates a challenge when it becomes normal for your team to bring everything to you for final review and approval. This is when a bottleneck happens, and everything grinds to a halt waiting for your sign off. So, what can you do to make it better?

How do you know when you are letting others set your agenda, control your calendar, or manage you, rather than the other way around? In other words, how do you reclaim your own *personal leadership*?

A few thoughts...

First, look at your calendar for the last 30-60 days.

Were the appointments set by you and based on your priorities or were they set in reaction to requests from others? What was discussed in those meetings-- your priorities or someone else's?

Look at your output and activity the last 30-60 days. Does it reflect your priorities, or those of others?

As the leader, you will need to spend *some* time coaching others, helping them overcome obstacles, and answering questions. Were those the purposes of your meetings or were you unintentionally doing someone else's work?

Second, stop and review the help you provided.

In those cases where you were answering someone's questions, helping them make a decision, or working through some obstacle, ask yourself why these matters rose to the level of your having to get involved.

Is it a training problem with your team? Do they understand the agency's mission and how their work supports it? Are they facing significant, unanticipated problems that only you and your experience can resolve? Have you not delegated to them the level of authority to handle these issues on their own? Are you doing an adequate job training, equipping, and empowering your team? In other words, could all these interruptions be telling you something about an opportunity to improve your leadership?

Once you honestly answer these questions for yourself, you will have a better idea of how to free yourself up from unnecessary distractions and stay focused on your priorities and those things that only you can do...that only you "own".

Third, recognize that the solution might be a bit tough to swallow.

To solve this challenge (freeing yourself up to work on your priorities) you will need to know yourself, understand the skill levels, shortcomings, and unique talents of your team, become effective at delegating authority and *decision-making power* (not just tasks) to them, and setting appropriate boundaries for the future.

There are some decisions only you as the leader should make, some that members of your team should make (without you), and those that should be made with your recommendations or brought to you for discussion. The better your team members become at decision-making, the more you can delegate to them. This helps them grow and frees you up to do what only you should be doing.

Do you know what it is that you — *and only you* — should be doing? Are you aware of the most important priorities you face as a leader?

If you find yourself struggling to answer this question, don't worry. We've all been there, and the next section should help.

The 9 Primary Responsibilities of a Nonprofit Leader

There are nine key responsibilities each leader must *own* as a part of their role in leading a nonprofit. If you want to help your organization get to the next level, achieve your mission, and make a bigger impact, it is critical that you understand and embrace these nine responsibilities.

Now, before you set fire to this book, abandoning all hope for change, I know what you're thinking… You're currently handling way more than nine responsibilities.

I get it. I've been there and I know you have a lot more on your plate. But hear me out for a minute….

You can try and handle all 317 responsibilities you're currently juggling, or you can give me a chance to introduce a new perspective. I promise, I'll help you get there, and there will be a light at the end of the tunnel.

So, what are these 9 Primary Responsibilities?

1. Protect the Vision

An agency's vision is an aspirational statement describing what your organization would like to see happen in the future. Everything the agency does and all decisions it makes should be in support of their vision.

Example Vision Statement: A world where everyone has a decent place to live. (Habitat for Humanity)

It is the role of the agency leader to protect the vision from being misused or ignored. As an ambassador, the leader shares the vision with others and ensures all agency decisions are aligned with the vision. What is your agency's Vision Statement? Do you have one?

Are your services and programs aligned with the Vision? Is there anything that should be changed? Is your team spending their time on tasks that relate to the Vision? Do you make it a priority to review programs, services, events, etc., on a regular basis to ensure they align with the Vision? What changes do you need to make to better lead toward the Vision?

2. Align with the Mission

A Mission Statement answers the question of why an agency exists or what it does on a higher level. It describes the *specific role* the agency plays in support of the vision statement and captures what the board believes it is called to do. It is an overview of what an agency does day-in and day-out and serves as a compelling rallying point for the staff, board, volunteers, supporters, and others.

Example Mission Statement: Seeking to put God's love into action, Habitat for Humanity brings people together to build homes, communities and hope. (Habitat for Humanity)

For many agencies, the Mission Statement often encompasses the reason the organization was initially founded. The leader's responsibility is to ensure the mission still applies and that everything the agency does is in support of the mission statement.

The Mission Statement should be long enough to include the primary objectives of the agency, yet short enough that it can be easily remembered by each person on the team. It serves as a guiding light for all key decisions — including setting top priorities, goals, creating budgets, defining organizational structure, board and staff recruiting and hiring preferences, and even solving day-to-day problems.

Agency leaders are responsible to align all resources, goals, budgets, recruiting, activities, and each part of the organization in a way that achieves its mission. For a leader, decision-making actually becomes much easier — *even when faced with one of those tough calls* — when you reread your mission statement and make your decisions in context.

When you teach your team (leaders and staff) to refer to the Mission Statement when making decisions, you empower them to solve problems without always seeking your opinion or needing approval to move forward.

Why is having a clear Mission Statement so important?

At a high level, it provides clarity for the leader, helping to make decision-making and day-to-day problem solving easier. It makes it much easier to say "no" to some potentially great ideas if they don't align with where the agency is headed. This will save time, allowing you to focus on more important initiatives.

A clear Mission Statement sets the tone and serves as an overall guide for the entire agency. It reminds board members, employees, volunteers, and donors exactly why the agency was created in the first place.

It makes decision-making (for everyone) much easier. If some activity or program is outside the scope of the mission, it should not be acted upon, planned for, or budgeted for. New programs and services that do not support the mission should be avoided.

It takes personal agenda's out of most decisions since the mission statement is a fixed marker. New ideas clearly either support the mission or not.

It helps set better goals and create more meaningful budgets because both must be crafted to support the mission. It also helps to focus everyone on the work at hand by ensuring efficient use of resources, towards specific, agreed upon goals. It helps eliminate problems and conflicts.

How do you know if your mission statement is clear and understood by others?

If you've never said "no" to a new idea, your mission statement is probably unclear or misunderstood. "Mission Creep" is allowing new ideas and tasks to be roped in to an original project or initiative. This has a significant impact on the budget and can drastically impact the ability of a team to hit an agreed-upon goal or timeline.

When you ask individuals on your team what your mission is, you get a variety of answers. Your team — including volunteers and board members — should be able to easily explain the mission and how their role relates to the bigger picture.

Decision-making becomes hard, and even sometimes contentious. Making decisions without a clear understanding and shared commitment to a future goal can be an exercise in futility. Each person will make a decision based on what is best for them or their team at the time. This can create bigger problems down the road.

Diagram your organization. Do one or more programs not clearly fit in? Do they look like orphans that you try and explain or defend? Are they detached from your main operations?   - As leader, you are constantly asked to make decisions others should clearly be making within their own authority.

I once had the opportunity to serve as a director and board chair for a nonprofit in the social service space. Not long after my time had ended, I learned they were approached by a major potential donor. He wanted to make a six-figure donation for each of the next three years.

On the surface it seemed like a great opportunity, but this particular donor had very specific instructions on how the money should be spent. After significant discussion, the board chose to deny the generous offer as it would have required the agency to expand its programming well beyond their current comfort level. It also didn't closely align with the mission or vision of the organization. It took some guts, but it was the right call.

It can be difficult — especially in the nonprofit world, where donations are the lifeblood of an agency — to turn down an opportunity like this. After all, six-figure donors don't come along every day. The board and leader of the nonprofit demonstrated strong character and commitment to what was most important — delivering on the existing mission of the agency.

Have you ever found yourself in this situation? Thing about what you might do if you were. Is your mission strong enough?

What is your agency's Mission Statement? Do you have one?

Are your services and programs aligned with the Mission? Is there anything that should be changed? Is your team spending their time on tasks that relate to the Mission? Do you make it a priority to review programs, services, events, etc. on a regular basis to ensure they align with the Mission? What changes do you need to make to better lead in line with the Mission?

3. Embrace and Enforce the Values

Think of values as your agency's ground rules or guidelines — defining how everyone associated with the agency is expected to conduct themselves. This applies both internally and externally. They play a critical role in protecting and maintaining your agency's culture. The leader's responsibility is to protect the culture by living out and reinforcing the values, calling out value violations, and recognizing those who follow them.

To make that a reality, you must do two things:

First, personally (and consistently) live out the values each and every day as everyone takes their cue from the leader. What you say, how you conduct yourself, and how consistently you call out violations by others is huge.

Second, clearly define each value so everyone understands what each of your agency values means and what they look like in your agency when people follow, or violate, one of them.

Without an agreed upon set of values to establish clear expectations of behavior and the manner of how things get done, you run the risk of having a *Wild West* approach to how people treat each other—a recipe for disaster.

What are your agency's values? Do you have any?

Is your culture a living breathing example of these values? Do you take every opportunity to act in accordance with the values? Do you reward actions and decisions made by your team, in line with the values? What changes do you need to make in your agency to bring values to the forefront?

4. Develop and/or Implement a Strategic Plan

A leader has a critical responsibility to see that the organization has a written and current strategic plan. It is a high-level outline of the top 3-5 priorities it intends to work on during the upcoming period, usually 2-3 years, to accomplish its mission. It is based on the organization's mission, vision, values, its expectation of conditions in the near future, and its assessment of its current internal capabilities.

The plan usually consists of the organization's mission statement, vision statement, values statement, key priorities, and SMART goals.

A leader has two responsibilities regarding strategic plans. The first is to ensure the agency *has* a workable strategic plan in place that sets a mutually agreed upon path to achieving the mission. Most will include 3-5 specific key priorities the agency will focus on to achieve the mission.

The second responsibility is to ensure all operations are in line with the plan and nothing is in conflict. All budgeting, decisions, marketing, hiring, programs, etc. must exist to support the agency's mission. Any that do not should be changed or eliminated.

Each strategy is intended to accomplish an important end in fulfillment of an agency's mission. For instance, an agency may have a fundraising strategy, a marketing strategy, a growth or expansion strategy, etc.

Without a strategy to unite everyone's efforts, thinking, and focus, an agency's well-intended team may inadvertently end up working against each other.

Does Your Agency Have a Strategic Plan? Is it Current?

Are you satisfied with the Strategic Plan and how it is being implemented? Does everyone on your team know about it? Is it on track for completion on time or are some areas falling behind? How often do you measure progress on the plan? What are some of the key objectives in the plan?

5. Manage the Agency-Board Relationship

One of the most important roles a leader fulfills — and one that only he or she can do — is establishing and maintaining a collaborative and supportive relationship with the board. Just as important is the leader having a positive and effective working relationship with the board chair.

Without a solid basis of trust, transparency, and unity between the board, its chair, and you — the agency leader — all of you, including the agency, will be in for a rough road. If there is one single piece of advice I can share with you — to ensure a rewarding and effective working relationship with your board — this is it. *Stay close to you board and its chair.*

I am a firm believer the agency leader and board chair must stay in periodic communication, even between board meetings. The underlying philosophy should be, *No Surprises.* This doesn't mean *No Bad News.* That would be impossible. But what is possible and required is frank and full discussions, so everyone knows what's happening.

Boards have significant responsibility, including its fiduciary duty, so requests for additional details or greater clarity shouldn't be seen as invasive. They should carry special weight and be handled as quickly and efficiently as possible.

In cases where I have served as board chair, I always tried to meet with the executive director between board meetings to maintain open communication channels, support their efforts, and discuss the agendas of upcoming meetings.

One executive director I know records a brief board update video that is sent to each board member between meetings. This is a quick, effective way to inform directors of important goings-on between meetings.

Are You Effectively Managing the Agency/Board Relationship?

Do you meet with your board chair on a regular basis? Are you doing your best to provide your board with accurate and current information about things going on in the agency? Do you operate with a *No Surprises* mentality? What could you do to help improve the Agency/Board relationship?

6. Communicate. Communicate. Communicate.

Like it or not, you are the agency's "Communicator-in-Chief" for both internal and external audiences. Employees, volunteers, donors, community partners, foundations, other agencies, and a variety of other people all look to you for vision, direction, clarity, and leadership.

When leading staff meetings you will have to answer tough questions, especially if you are in the midst of leading internal organizational change. When speaking before community partners or other agencies the words you choose will carry significant weight, as they are *coming from the top*.

Seek to clarify whenever possible. There will always be people who are either misinformed or uninformed. They need the clarity only you can convincingly provide.

When people have general questions, or want to know about something specific, they will come to you. This is part of your role as a leader. It's always better to share as much of whatever information people are seeking, as possible. Where there is an information vacuum, people are will usually make assumptions and fill in the blanks on their own. You can get in front of this — and frame the story in the correct light — by sharing as much as possible.

You will also likely be called upon to answer the same question over and over, especially during times of change. Try to show as much patience as possible. Sometimes when people ask the same question, they aren't looking for information as much as they are looking for assurance. Your knowledge of the situation, and confidence in the process will help reassure them that change is a positive thing.

Are You Communicating as Much as Possible?

Do you regularly share updates with your leadership team, board, and employees? Do you provide opportunities for people to ask follow-up questions when needed? How can you find ways to share more?

7. Maintaining Key External Relationships

Agencies typically work with many individuals, businesses, and other nonprofits in the community. While all relationships are important, some have may have taken on an elevated importance when it comes to your agency's success. Those are the vital relationships you have with many key individuals and organizations in your community.

These may include major donors, former directors, community leaders, community services organizations, foundation leaders, and nonprofit association leaders. These are special relationships built up over the years by working together. Treat them as precious assets of your agency.

Someone has to "own" these relationships and see that they are properly tended. That responsibility primarily falls to you, but you may choose to have someone on your team help support these relationships if properly prepared ahead of time. One of your most important roles as the leader is serving as the "face of the agency" to outside constituents.

There will be times when you can delegate the task of a phone call or outside presentation to a development director, marketing manager, or community advocate, but for the most part, these are your responsibility. Everyone wants to hear from the leader.

While I loved this part of leadership when I was a CEO in the for-profit world, as a board chair of a nonprofit, I felt the executive director should be the face of the agency. The development director should be a close second. When appropriate we would make presentations together as community groups also like to speak with volunteers — including board members.

Are You Maintaining Key External Relationships?

Do you regularly engage with people that may be able to help the organization? Are you aware of who these people are? Do you make a point of meeting with vital donors, past directors, or community leaders? Is there anything you should be doing to improve on your current efforts?

8. Building the Best, Collaborative, Talented Team Possible

When I became a CEO I knew right way that neither I or the company could succeed unless the team succeeded. I remember chairing my first leadership team meeting. It was humbling to realize that almost every person in that room was much better than me, in at least one key area.

It can be tempting for a leader to be jealous or feel threatened of the skills and talents around them. Fortunately, I was able to embrace them knowing they were exactly the kind of team you need to build a successful organization.

If you're like most leaders, you're probably a take charge kind of person, but remember no one can do it it all on their own. Even if you are blessed with a unique and varied set of competencies — and recognized as such — your role is to lead, not *do*.

Your job is to identify, recruit, hire, and lead the best talent you can find to fill out your leadership team and staff. Period.

Humility and knowing yourself — both mentioned earlier — come into play here. To lead successfully, you should be honest with yourself, lead from your strengths, and hire people around you to fill in for your weaknesses.

For me, that has always been the financial skills part. Over the years I've learned to be pretty good at reviewing and analyzing financial reports. But there are many out there who are much better and quicker than I at determining what the financial result are telling us. I made a practice of seeking out individuals with that skill set — to help me and the rest of the team — understand our financial data.

We also had a great need for improved IT performance. Our system was old, slow, and did not give us the information we needed. However, we had a lot of self-anointed *IT experts* on staff who felt they knew exactly what we needed.

Our IT function was out of touch and we had a lot of people telling us what to do. We wasted a lot of time and money until we found a terrific IT leader who actually listened to everyone and eventually came back with a terrific solution to our problems.

Find the right people, hire them, tell them what you need done, and get out of their way. It's the best thing you can do.

I was blessed with several gifted individuals who led important departments. There was no way I could have ever reached the skill level they had. They had not only my confidence but — just as importantly — the confidence of the rest of the leadership team. Building a team of individuals — each gifted in their own areas — is the most effective way to ensure the success of any organization.

Are You Building the Best Team Possible?

Have you spent time reviewing your strengths and weaknesses? Do you know which people you have on your team now that complement the areas where you struggle? Have you identified the additional skills and talents you need, to push your Strategic Plan forward? Do you regularly engage with your key team members to learn more about them and help with their professional development? Is there anything you can do to improve your team building skills?

9. Be Around, But Not in The Way

We've covered eight key leadership principles. You've had a chance to think about all the ways your effective leadership can help improve your organization. You want to dive right in, but right now you may be asking yourself a big question…

"How do I stay focused on what really matters, what should I be doing first, and how do I get out of all the other 'stuff' I'm already involved in?"

Great question. First things first, remember, you can't do it all. Yes, it bears repeating. *No matter how amazing you are as a leader — and I know you are — you still can't do it all.*

Should you ignore your other responsibilities to work on these core leadership principles? Should you dump things on your team and hope for the best? While I admit, these first two are tempting, they will likely lead to bigger issues down the road.

The best advice I can give you is to be around but get out of the way. The idea is not to abandon your team, but also create healthy boundaries that encourage them to solve problems and think on their own.

To make it easier, you can follow these five steps:

1. Ensure you have a Vision, Mission, and Values.
2. Get clear about roles — yours and theirs.
3. Delegate (for real) — Using the 5-step system.
    - - - Get prepared.
    - - - Paint a picture.
    - - - Provide background (and a why).
    - - - Be clear about expectations.
    - - - Allow for questions.
4. Get out of the way.
5. Support… with boundaries.

How can you put these 5 steps into action? Let's dig a little deeper into each one and what's involved.

1. Ensure you have a Vision, Mission, and Values.

This can be something as simple as a one-page document, but it needs to be clear. Where you headed (ultimately), what role does your agency plan in achieving this goal, and what type of culture do you have? If you don't have these things, or if you do but they aren't clear to your team, you can forget about steps 2-5. No matter how much you try to delegate, the team will still come back to you to make decisions, because they don't know the bigger picture.

2. Get clear about roles — yours and theirs.

Take a few minutes to think about your Vision, Mission, and Values, and ideally your Strategic Plan. What role do you want to play in moving the agency forward? Do you need to more fully embrace any of the 9 Key Leadership Responsibilities? If so, what will you give up? What role do you need to play, and as a result, what roles do your team members need to play? Which responsibilities should be yours, and which should be theirs?

3. Delegate (for real) — Using the 5-step system.

For some people delegation comes easy. If you're like the rest of us, it can prove tricky at times. One of the keys to successful delegation is to make sure you're delegating *decision-making* as well as tasks. If you only hand off tasks, you're only free to focus on your role until a decision needs to be made. You need to make sure you've communicated the bigger picture, so people know *how* what they are doing fits into the bigger plan. Before you hand off your next text, take a few minutes and follow this *5 Step Delegation System*.

A. Get prepared.

Think through what you're trying to delegate, what needs to get done, the end result you want, who the best person for the job is, and if they will actually have the information, tools, and skills to get the job done successfully. If you can't answer that question, you might want to do a bit more planning before the hand off.

B. Paint a picture.

When delegating a responsibility or task, paint a picture of what a successful end result looks like. Allow your team to ask questions until they fully understand it.

C. Provide background (and a why).

Explain to your team why this task or responsibility is important, and how it fits into the bigger picture. No one wants to waste their time on things that don't matter.

D. Be clear about expectations.

How long do you expect the task to take? When do you expect the project done? What is the budget you expect to stay within? Do you expect them to work with anyone else? Are there obstacles or hurdles they might meet? How do you expect them to deal with them? And most importantly, set expectations for communication. Should they ask you when they have a question? Save all questions for a weekly check-in meeting? Send an email for more information? By communicating expectations up front you can eliminate unneeded frustration later.

E. Allow for questions.

This one part of the puzzle can make or break you when delegating tasks or responsibilities. Many leaders make the assumption their team understands what they have been assigned. Don't assume. Let me repeat. Don't assume. Until you've given people a chance to ask questions and build their own understanding of a project, task, or responsibility, you cannot assume it matches yours.

With each conversation give your team members an opportunity to clarify and ask questions. Do your best to remain patient and answer each question with as much information as possible. Remember, this will save you headaches later.

4. Get out of the way.

No, this doesn't mean abandoning them, or locking yourself in your office with a sign on the door that says *Important Meeting in Progress*. You should be available as needed, so they don't end up feeling like they are alone. But you can create boundaries and be a bit less available. Establishing healthy boundaries around decision-making will tell your team just how far they can do, especially if you are unavailable.

To help your team adjust to you being *less around* you will want to communicate your intent to make changes. Simply not showing up at the office one day — *without telling them ahead of time* — could create concern or panic. Not helpful if your goal is to empower them.

Get any from the day-to-day noise and activity around the agency periodically. Spend some quiet time looking at and analyzing your agency from the 50,000-foot level. Try to spot trends, subtle changes, how things seem to be going generally. What do you see? Which areas need attention, which ones are doing well?

If someone wanted to acquire or merge with your agency, what concerns would they have? How would they see your organization? These types of questions can help your mind transition from the day-to-day to higher level thinking. They can also help you stay out of things you assigned to others on your team. Remember, if you're going to go through all the effort of successfully delegating, so you be the leader you were designed to be, *you have to let go and get out of the way.*

5. Support… with boundaries.

For some leaders, setting specific times for questions or providing information, helps everyone focus more and accomplish their tasks. Your team won't bring you questions every other minute if they know they can get undivided attention during a particular block of time.

Develop your team leaders and delegate to them as much authority as you possibly can and empower them to act. Remember *Trust but Verify*. It's important to trust your team to deliver on the results you expect, but it's always a good idea to have a system setup to provide insight into project progress, etc.

During my leadership time in the for-profit world, I often practiced MBWA — Management by Walking Around. I spent time each week walking around the offices chatting with people informally, both about the work and life in general. I wanted to stay close to them because, first of all — they were really neat people, and second — they were the ones actually doing most of the work. I wanted to see if things were actually proceeding as I believed or had been told. Once in a while, I'd learn something that didn't match up with other information I had so it gave me a chance to do some digging.

How Will You be Around, But Not in The Way?

What steps should you take to refocus your daily routine onto the most critical areas in your agency? What can you delegate to others? What do you routinely, almost automatically do, that you should stop doing immediately? What should you start doing immediately?

Leading a nonprofit can be one of the most difficult and daunting roles. Leading for ultimate impact and getting your agency to the next level can seem almost impossible. But I promise you, you can do it. If can embrace the 9 Primary Responsibilities of a Leader, you *can* make positive change happen.

They aren't easy, but they are worth it. As you begin to work on these responsibilities you will not only see positive change in your agency, but you will be delightfully surprised in the positive changes you see in yourself and your team.

Are you ready to lead better?

PART 2:

LEADING THE ORGANIZATION

CHAPTER 4

Leadership: The Best of The Best

Great leaders aren't born, they are created.

Everyone wants to think that the greatest leaders we all look up to were born that way. And sure, some people may be born with character traits and/or personalities that lend themselves more to leadership.

Did you take it upon yourself to organize *everyone's* crayons in preschool? Did you self-appoint to the leader of the drinking fountain line? Then you might have some natural leadership tendencies. Of course, you might also have some control freak tendencies — most great leaders do... But that's for another book. The point is, anyone can become a good leader, no matter where they began.

I firmly believe that great leaders are not born, they are created. Whatever level your leadership is now, it can be better. You *can* be exactly the leader you want to be. How?

Success leaves clues. I've always loved this simple yet not-so-simple concept. If you want to be a great leader, you don't have to recreate the wheel. The cave men already did it for you. You just have to look at what they did, and repeat, ideally skipping the things that didn't work, thereby shortcutting your own road.

To make it easier for you, I've distilled decades of leadership practice, and dozens of leadership books, into the 7 leadership principles I believe are the most critical for nonprofit leaders.

1. Make all decisions consistent with the agency's Mission, Vision and Values.

We discussed this in great detail earlier. If you need a quick refresher, skip back to Part 1 - Chapter 3. Your agency will do amazingly well if you remain locked in on your purpose and the values (ground rules) you follow in achieving your mission.

Doing everything — *especially making decisions* — in light of your Mission, Vision, and Values makes you a responsible steward of the resources your agency has been given. From time to time you will be held responsible to others — donors, foundations, governmental bodies, etc. for how you managed those resources (people, funds, gifts-in-kind, etc.). Staying focused on your mission will make this much easier.

Even financial decisions should be made in light of the Mission, Vision, and Values. Most agencies have little wiggle room in their budgets and cannot afford to make major financial mistakes. Whereas huge organizations have bigger budgets and can usually recover from a well-intended decision that somehow went bad financially. Staying consistent and within the outline of your Mission Statement can help you stay focused and avoid costly mistakes.

Your budgets, goals, hiring practices, marketing, and behaviors should all be consistent *all the time*. If you let marketing do whatever they want but hold client services to specific standards in line with the mission, it will kill your message, hurt your credibility and ultimately negatively impact your ability to distinguish your agency from others in the community.

Need an example? What pet projects does your agency still fund and support that just seem to never die but go on and on without adding any significant value to the agency? These could be out of line with the Mission.

2. Stay focused on what your clients need *today* to succeed, not on what they needed when your agency was first created and ensure you are addressing the current needs.

Ask yourself, if your agency didn't exist and you were building it today for the first time, would it be organized the same way as it is now, offering the same services as today?

Does your agency need a quick review to see if it is still relevant? How can you make that happen? If your agency did not exist and you were building it today for the first time, would it be organized the same way as today, offering the same services as today?

3. Establish ideal indicators to measure progress.

It's not enough anymore to just count how many people your agency fed, clothed, or even attend your church each week. Boards and donors want to know output, results, and impact.

How many people now have jobs, how many people now have a roof over their heads, how many animals have you placed in new homes? What metrics do you use to measure success?

4. Understand the difference between costs and investments.

By default, most nonprofits look at every cost as an expense — even those that will add value to the agency. Training, automation improvements, donor management programs, phone systems, client management systems, and conference and workshop attendance are just a few.

I think one reason this happens is that leaders fall into the *volunteer trap*. They often have the luxury of engaging many volunteers. Perhaps the thinking is..."Why invest in these systems when I have all these no cost volunteers here to handle things manually?" Nonprofit leaders are also generally under pressure from many different sides to cut costs — especially costs that may not relate directly to services provided.

It's easy to fall into this line of thinking — but you can't ignore the hard truth. Inefficiency always costs something in terms of both hard costs and soft costs. Think about the costs an agency incurs due to late or inaccurate reporting, haphazard or incomplete donor record keeping, or the inability to find your data to complete grant requests.

What important investments have not made it to your budget but could significantly improve your operations? How can you approach others to get them approved this year?

5. Take time to work on your agency, not just in it.

As Michael Gerber suggests in *The E Myth Revisited*, try to pull yourself out of your day to day routine once in a while and critically assess the condition and functionality at your agency from the 50,000-foot level. What do you see? Are all systems working properly? If it were a business, would you want to buy it, or merge with it? Look at is as if it were for sale; is it marketable? What would make it more attractive to others?

6. Remember to focus on the agency's future and on the external world in which it works.

What does this mean? It's very easy to become consumed by the busyness of the here and now and forget to think long term. Short term thinking may yield better short-term results but will surely hurt the agency's performance and existence long term.

The same holds true for your agency's inner workings. It's so easy to become consumed and distracted by your internal processes, and everything going on, that you forget you need to be out in the community creating or nurturing relationships, telling your agency's story, and building more support for your cause. What could you be doing to get out in the community more?

7. Ask great questions.

As the leader, you may be pretty far removed from the agency's day to day details. It's critical that you ask the right people the right questions, so you know if your agency is on track for success.

What are the right questions? That depends on how your agency is doing and where it is on the life cycle. You may want to try some of the following:

- Are we on track with our Strategic Plan goals? *If not, why?*
- What do our clients want most from us?
- What things should we stop doing NOW?
- What things should we start doing NOW?
- What must we protect at all costs?
- What must we continue doing?

If you focus on these 7 Key Leadership Principles, you will help keep your organization on the right track. You will be an informed leader, ready to take action when needed and make better decisions.

CHAPTER 5

Leading Your Team

Be the Leader they are compelled to follow.

I learned a lot in my first leadership role — most of it the hard way. I made mistakes, got knocked down, brushed myself off and kept trying. It's the way many of us learn. But hopefully I can make your journey a little easier…

If you want your team to follow you — by choice, there are a few key things you need to embrace in your leadership.

Be generous and open with your praise and stingy with your reprimands.

I became aware of "One Minute Praisings" from Ken Blanchard and Spencer Johnson's book *The One Minute Manager*. I wish I'd found it a lot earlier. There is a simple yet elegant magic in taking a minute to praise or thank someone in public for a job well done.

Don't just send an email or text, but instead recognize them at a team meeting or other public setting. It doesn't have to be fancy, formal, or financial. Just a few words to recognize a job well done, a good idea, or a problem solved, will go a long way.

When someone needs a reprimand, the authors suggest a one-minute reprimand, done privately, quickly, and with clarity on what the issue is. Again, this coaching technique is powerful, allowing you to get your message out to the individual without embarrassing or berating them.

Invest in and build your team through a regular program of training and development.

Training, coaching, mentoring, and developing your team is a leader's primary responsibility and the key to making your agency more relevant and dynamic, as well as making your own job easier. Even in tough times, you'll find keeping these programs will lead to a much more successful agency.

You've probably heard the story of the CFO who asked his CEO, "Why do we spend so much time and money on training when some people leave?" The CEO responded and said, "What if we don't train them and they stay?"

Training and development of people is not an option. Not only does it help your team build new skills, increasing their value to the organization, but the confidence boost as a result of learning new skills will do wonders for your overall morale.

At one point during my tenure as CEO for a large firm, we developed an assessment tool called TalentScapes. Its purpose was to learn three things about each of those individuals we considered our high potential/high value team members.

1. Were they satisfied with their current position and their growth opportunities or might we lose them to another company so they could continue to grow professionally?
2. Do we have adequate personnel back-up if any of our high capacity people left us?
3. What areas within the organization would they like to be exposed to so they could learn more about the big picture of the organization.

For those wanting to expand their horizons, we intentionally gave them new opportunities to work on important cross-functional teams within other departments on nontypical projects. It was big hit. We were able to develop our next tier of top performers through important and interesting assignments.

Not only did the team respond positively and engage on a whole new level, but by bringing people from different departments together to work on a problem you gain new ideas and fresh insight.

Who in your agency do you need to start developing by delegating to and investing in their skills and confidence?

Develop and practice your communication skills.

One skill every successful agency leader must have is the ability to communicate effectively. Leaders are the face of the agency and are often invited to speak to outside groups to share their vision and goals — including donors, foundations, and others.

They also frequently speak at internal team meetings, where the audience is watching the leader's tone, every word choice, and even every nuanced gesture — some which can communicate far more than just what the leader is saying.

Leadership expert Max De Pree once said the leader is the agency's Chief Reality Officer. People look to them for facts, honesty, and to "call 'em as he sees 'em".

Leaders must speak truth, never lie, and always be trusted. Most people understand certain information must be kept confidential. When these occasions arise, you can tell them you are not free to share it, at that time, but may be able to do so later.

People want clear, consistent, and frequent messages from the leader, especially during times of change, uncertainty, or reorganization. I found speaking frequently to our team, using consistent language and using simple, clear words helped me get my message across. When leaders use fancy words designed to impress the audience, it usually back fires and makes the situation worse.

People want honesty from their leader so an upfront, even if at times embarrassing "I don't know" can be so refreshing to hear. Always be yourself. A little genuine vulnerability can speak volumes to your team and earn their respect.

Part of my personal communication strategy as a leader has always included MBWA—*managing by walking around*. If you lead a large organization, you will be amazed by how much you learn by occasionally wandering around and asking questions.

I also hosted a monthly "Breakfast with Tom" where we'd invite people, usually by department, to meet with me for an hour for a continental breakfast so they could ask me any questions, with nothing off limits. They were great at helping the team get a peek behind the leadership curtain and to dispel rumors before they began.

I also hosted an ice cream party once when we were going through a particularly challenging time. The team needed to know we were OK, that I knew what they were going through, and that I appreciate their fortitude.

Communicating with your team on a regular basis isn't the only part of communication that is important for a leader. You also need to continually hone your skills as a polished speaker outside of the organization. Remember, you are the face of the agency and will likely find yourself in many situations where you will be telling the agency story, often with little time to prepare. Professional training in this area can help.

Early in my career, I joined The Toastmasters Organization. It helped me gain poise and taught me how to organize and present a speech. It also helped me to be more comfortable in front of an audience.

How do you rate your communication skills? Where are you strongest, weakest? What steps can you take to improve over the next six months?

Try to maintain a controlled sense of urgency.

A little healthy friction or discomfort can ensure the right things are being done, being done well, and in a timely manner. In some organizations — especially larger agencies — process and culture can slow things down so much that nothing seems to get done. By setting appropriate but challenging deadlines and keeping things moving forward you can keep your team focused on getting things done.

Always put the momentum ball back in their court. When speaking with your team as a whole or one-on-one, don't let yourself be the reason progress on a project stalls out. Always ensure they know the next steps to take are theirs and that you are there to encourage, support, and help them, but it is their job to do. If you aren't careful, you can easily become responsible for everybody else's work.

What can you do to help ignite a controlled sense of urgency in your organization?

Create cross-functional teams when possible.

When you need to tackle a big problem, create a team made up of someone from each of your key areas. The cross-training everyone will receive by working on the project together will be invaluable. They will all come away with a better understanding of the entire agency, not just their individual area.

Not only will this will create better relationships, but it will help things run smoother over time. They will probably even come up with a better result than if you just keep the original team on the project.

Keep things simple.

Leading a nonprofit isn't easy, but there are things you can do to make it simpler. You can bring simplicity to the agency by ensuring everything you do stems from your mission, vision, and values.

If you maintain tight alignment between your strategic priorities, goals, budgets, projects, external messaging, hiring practices, and key partnerships, it will be much easier for others to embrace who you are and what you are doing. Inconsistencies between any of these will be obvious to others and significantly slow down your progress.

When holding team meetings, try out the following:

- Always provide updates on goals/priorities
- Always take at least a few questions
- Always refocus everyone on the mission and what you are doing so they don't forget the *critical success factors*

What can you do to simplify your agency and better align with the Vision, Mission, and Values?

Embrace Servant Leadership.

Leadership is a privilege, not a right. No matter how you came to be in your position, if you want your team to follow you, you will have to *earn* their respect. One of the most effective ways to do this, is to adopt the characteristics of a *Servant Leader*.

As described by Skip Pritchard and Audrey Malpers — their models for leadership outline how to lead effective in today's culture. Your team will work harder for you and deliver community impact like you've never seen, if you lead from the heart. What does a Servant Leader do?

- They value diverse opinion—not just "yes-men".
- They cultivate a culture of trust.
- They develop other leaders.
- They encourage their team members.
- They think long term, not just in the moment.

- They act with humility.
- They make others feel valued in their roles.
- They bring out the best in others, by empowering them.
- They very seldom use power and/or authority as leverage.
- They know what to focus on — the important, rather than getting sucked into the urgent, but less important.
- They are a resource to others, not just their boss. They are there to help others do their job, not the other way around.

Remember, when someone has a challenge inhibiting their progress, your job is to support their efforts and help them through the process, not rescue them. Most people don't actually want you to solve their problems for them. They want to be given the knowledge and tools needed to deal with the challenge and empowered to make decisions and solve problems on their own.

When you lead your team in this way you will not only be building their problem-solving skills, but you will be developing them so they can handle more in the future and building their confidence.

Embracing these 7 Key Leadership Principles will help you be a more effective leader, develop your team, and enable your organization to make a bigger impact.

But in a nonprofit, you're not only leading your team, you're also leading your "invisible workforce" — your volunteers.

In the next chapter we'll talk about what you need to do to effectively lead your extended team.

CHAPTER 6

Leading Your *Volunteer* Team

Be the leader they're inspired to follow.

In a typical (for-profit) company leaders only have to be concerned with one kind of team — their employees or direct reports. Each person in the organization is directly incentivized (through their paychecks) to work to the best of their abilities and complete the tasks and goals they are given. The high-level consequences of not completing work are generally clear — out they go. Of course, it's never quite that simple, but at least the ground rules are there.

But in a non-profit you have an even tougher job. Not only do you have to manage and motivate your paid employees, but you have another team — an *invisible* workforce — your volunteers.

Depending on the size and scope of your organization you may have a multitude or only a few, but nearly every nonprofit has at least some volunteers. This team can often be the lifeblood of a nonprofit — without them you might not survive….

Your volunteers are your most authentic ambassadors, your unsung heroes, and more often than not, the face of your organization. They are the ones that often come through in a pinch, throwing in their efforts shoulder to shoulder along with your paid team members... And they are doing it all simply for the good of the mission. Ok, a few may be doing it to pad a resume, or gain experience, or other personal reasons, but for the most part they are there simply because the cause — your cause — matters. That's powerful stuff.

On top of being driven by a great purpose rather than a paycheck, what I find even more interesting is this invisible workforce is growing. The desire to get involved and volunteer is on the rise. People want to make a difference. They want to be a part of something bigger than themselves, for a purpose far more impactful than the all-mighty dollar.

Whether it's recent retirees, those who are no longer content just being successful in their careers and want to do something significant for others, or purpose-driven millennials, many people with substantial skills are exploring ways nonprofits can fulfill their desire to help.

Some people see their community members going through tough times. Some may have been helped when they went through difficulties themselves and are driven to "pay it forward." Students have community service hours to fulfill. Whatever the reason, they're out there and looking for meaningful ways to serve.

At the same time, many nonprofits have their own challenges. Every nonprofit is trying to get its name and message out to anyone who will listen. Budgets are very tight, leaving agencies little to invest in infrastructure. Often each payment out is viewed as an expense rather than an investment. Donations rarely grow as quickly as the demand for services. Top level nonprofit talent is being targeted and often recruited away by other agencies. Government financial support is uncertain, even when budgeted and promised.

Agencies are generally unable to hire staff or consultants with specialized skills that can help the agency succeed. They often rely on volunteer help to fill much of the need in the organization.

Many people think of volunteers as those who help hold down costs, but smart leaders know volunteers are a valuable piece of the organization and spend time and effort nurturing that resource.

There are three common and ***significant*** problems nonprofit leaders have when it comes to volunteers.

1. They don't know where to find more volunteers.

2. They don't know how to *value* volunteers — how to make them feel appreciated so they continue to give their best each day and continue serving.

3. They often don't have a written Volunteer Program or Philosophy.

Here are a few questions to ask yourself to see if any of these challenges are present in your organization.

- Do you consistently and strategically recruit volunteers based on specific need or do you just take anyone interested that walks through your doors?
- Do you interview new volunteer candidates to determine "fit" and best use?
- Do you have an orientation and training program for new volunteers?
- Do you make a point of regularly showing your appreciation for all the work your volunteers do?
- Do you have a Volunteer Coordinator (even if only part-time)?

If your answer to any (or most) of these questions is yes, you might have some of the top three volunteer challenges. But there's hope. There are things you can do right now to improve your volunteer situation.

How to find more (good) volunteers.

Volunteers are like revenue: they don't just show up. You have to be intentional and look for them. Much like finding new board candidates, identifying high-value volunteers is a year-round job.

Keep in mind, a general request for volunteer help isn't likely to get you the exact type of help you need. It can also run the risk of confusing those you ask. You must be specific in your requests.

Example: Do you need help developing content for social media? Then you need to find a web-based copywriter with a passion for saving dogs. Your friend's brother Bob, who happens to work as a graphic designer for a marketing company isn't likely to be a good fit. You'll both end up frustrated and you'll probably lose his help in the end. However, if you need help designing your annual report or creating images for your website, Bob might be just the guy.

Think of recruiting volunteers just as you would recruiting for a paid position. Stop and think through the specific *results* or you need out of a future volunteer and the skills and/or talents that would help them achieve those results.

You don't need to write a two-page job description, but a few key points about the help you need, the skills or experience you're looking for, and the culture (overall feel) of the agency will go a long ways into helping you recruit quality volunteers and save time weeding through those that don't match your needs.

Remember to also think about the time commitment you might need from the volunteer. Is this for a specific two-month project, where you need 10 hours a week, but it's over in June? Do you need 25 volunteers for a large event during a weekend, or perhaps someone to serve in the soup kitchen 4 hours a month on an ongoing basis.

Potential volunteers are exceedingly busy — just like the rest of us. While they want to give their time, it's critical to have clear expectations about what you need so you can be sure it's a good fit for both sides.

Assuming you've spent some time, thinking through your volunteer needs, how can you go about finding great volunteers? As someone who has been on both the recruiting volunteers and the volunteering side, I have a few suggestions.

- Step into the shoes of a potential volunteer and go digging. Do a little research online for "volunteer opportunities" or volunteer matching. There are a many websites that will attempt to match specific nonprofits with volunteers. Many of these will allow nonprofits to post a volunteer need for free.

- Check your local community website or any local foundation's website, for a feature connecting nonprofit agencies to would-be volunteers. Often these sites will help nonprofits by trying to connect individuals in the community with ways to serve.

- Join your Chamber of Commerce. Many nonprofit leaders belong to and actively participate in chamber groups or events as a way to network, gain community visibility, and recruit others. Getting involved will give you a chance to meet others that already have a desire to be involved in the community.

- Ask local high schools and colleges if they require service hours of their students. Your agency might be a good fit.

- Prominently post your *specific* volunteer needs

on your website's homepage and on social media, encouraging others to share. This can be a great way to identify a friend-of-a-friend.

- Look for opportunities to deliver presentations to community service organizations like the Rotary, Lion's Club, Kiwanis Club, Chamber of Commerce, or others and invite the attendees to visit your agency and consider volunteering.

- Ask your current volunteers to suggest names of potential volunteers or ask their friends about volunteering.

- Identify local businesses that have some form of either a professional development program for their high capacity talent or a community outreach program. If so, discuss ways to partner with them by providing meaningful community service opportunities. Keep an eye out for businesses interested in being associated with causes that fit your agency's overall mission.

  For example, some technology-based companies may have a strong interest in supporting education in the community. If your agency helps with literacy it might be a perfect fit. Many larger organizations list their values or beliefs on their website. This can be a great way to see if they might align with your agency.

- Reach out to the faith-based community through church bulletins, church websites, and the ministry of Care pastors in local churches.

- Ask your current and former board members for volunteer suggestions. Make a specific request and ask them to bring three names of candidates to the next board meeting.

- Advertise through your local community career centers, job assistance agencies, etc. Workers in transition often want to avoid a gap on their resume between jobs. Some will consider volunteering to stay active in the community, learn new skills, or build their network. This can be a great way to tap into great talent.

- Assess your current volunteers. Which ones do you consider the best? Where did they come from? Can you follow the same path to find more?

- Keep a list of good potential volunteers. When you meet someone that would make a great volunteer, or has special skills, etc. remember that individual. Connect with them online or at least write their name down. Even if you don't need their skills at the moment, they might be a good fit down the road. It will be much easier to draw from an existing pool when the need arises than it will be to go searching last minute.

You've defined the need, reached out through various methods, and done the impossible — you've recruited ten fantastic new volunteers for your organization. Now what?

How do you treat volunteers, so they stay motivated, feel appreciated, and most importantly — *stay* with your agency?

First things first. I'm guessing if you're leading a nonprofit volunteering is in your blood.

If you've never volunteered and you're leading a nonprofit organization, I highly suggest you take a day off and go volunteer a few times somewhere outside of your agency. You will learn more in a day or two volunteering than you will almost anywhere else.

But for now, we'll assume you have some volunteer experience. Let's think back to that time in college when your friend convinced you to help save the alligators. Remember that agency?

What was that like? How were you treated? Did you feel like a member of the team or just as a set of hands and feet to be used however they wanted? Did you feel valued? Did you have a sense of the big picture or were you just a cog somewhere in that big machine? Perhaps you've had multiple volunteer experiences.

What were some of the good ones and why? What were some of the bad and what made them bad?

What specific things did any of these agencies did

that made you feel special, or perhaps very un-special as a volunteer? What lessons did you learn that you can apply to your agency today?

This one might surprise you, but as a general rule of thumb, I believe you should treat your volunteers just like any other valuable paid team member. It's easy to fall into the trap of seeing them as "just volunteers." Don't do it. They should be treated the same as your employees and board members, except there is one *key* difference.

Your volunteers chose to be there and could be doing absolutely anything else with their time other than volunteering at your agency.

The most important thing to keep your volunteers choosing to spend their time with your organization is to make them feel appreciated and ensure they understand the value they are bringing to the organization.

What does that look like? Try a few of these.

- Treat your volunteers as your "partners" instead of just part-time workers. The reality is, many nonprofits could not survive without volunteers.

- Fully orient and train new volunteers, just like you would a full-time employee. In fact, preferable along with new employee hires.

- Review the agency's mission, vision, values,

any appropriate policies, and procedures. Don't just train them in the tasks you plan for them. Let them understand the big picture.

- Get to know them and learn what matters. Volunteers often have particular and individualized motivations (passion for the cause, giving back, meeting new people) for helping out. Your volunteer coordinator should meet with and interview each volunteer candidate to determine fit, skill sets, and the candidate's desires, to learn how best that person can be deployed at the agency, based on agency needs and the volunteer's preferences. Work to discover their motivators and what they enjoy doing and do whatever you can to help match that to a need in the organization.

- Include them in every staff meeting if possible; don't treat them like outsiders. Share information, share progress and share stories of impact from those you serve. Volunteers especially, want to know they are making a difference.

- Include them in all essential communications you send out and keep them up to date on the critical goings-on.

- Celebrate their service and thank them through luncheons, awards, etc. You don't have to spend a lot of money, but it is vital to show your appreciation for them in a real way.

- Remember that all volunteers could be doing other things, but they have chosen to spend some of their valuable time helping you carry out your mission. They should be treated respectfully and celebrated frequently.

- Host a volunteer appreciate party periodically to celebrate or recognize them at your gala.

- Freely share — in public — a one-minute praising when you catch them doing something special.

You've found the perfect volunteers. You're doing everything you can to show them how much they mean to your organization. Is there anything else you can do to successfully lead your *invisible workforce?*

Create a written Volunteer Program or Philosophy.

Develop a standard approach to volunteer involvement so everyone understands how volunteers are to be treated and used, and that both volunteers and staff understand exactly what is expected of them, how they are supposed to work together, and how they can best immerse themselves into the agency's culture and workflow.

Do you have a dedicated Volunteer Coordinator role, even a part-time position in your nonprofit? If your agency regularly uses multiple volunteers to achieve the mission, or even just to help out with administrative or back end office responsibilities, you need a Volunteer Coordinator. This person's key role is to help recruit, train, manage, and engage volunteers.

You may want to consider creating a Volunteer Policy Manual to ensure consistency in how volunteers are recruited, trained, and managed, as well as to show how important they are. This doesn't need to be complicated, but some simple published ground rules for the way your organization handles the volunteer program.

Remember to consistently show volunteers the respect and appreciation they deserve. Volunteers *do not* have to help you. If they're working full-time jobs, going to school, or taking care of a family, a Saturday afternoon with Netflix might be a lot more appealing than directing traffic for your festival on a 95-degree day in August.

Make every effort to embed and integrate each volunteer into the fiber of your agency. If they're helping because they're passionate about your cause, feeling like an outsider can be the quickest way to lose their interest.

Sit down with your volunteers periodically to get feedback. Ask if they still enjoy volunteering and find it rewarding and fulfilling. Ask if they feel like they are making a difference. Finally, ask them for ideas on how to improve services and operations. Listen to their feedback and try and find ways to use their suggestions to improve the volunteer experience.

Keep in mind, a spirit of volunteerism and the desire to give back or be involved in the community is embedded in the hearts of most individuals. With few exceptions we all want to help those in need and many of us feel the desire to be a part of something bigger and have a purpose beyond our day jobs.

Be bold and tap into that need whenever you talk to someone about your organization. They won't be offended and might even want to get involved. If they don't have time, they might know someone else.

Lastly, remember that it is a privilege and an honor to lead and serve volunteers. These are the people that are giving of their hearts, time, and potentially dollars — solely for the good of the mission. They don't get a paycheck they can't be fired. Treat them with respect. Value their contributions. Find ways to connect them to experiences that matter most to them. You will be amazed at the untapped potential of truly great volunteers.

In the next chapter we'll talk about some of the most significant volunteers you have — your board of directors — and how you can lead your board for impact.

PART 3:

LEADING THE BOARD

FROM THE INSIDE OUT

CHAPTER 7

Your Board's Role in the Organization

"The price of greatness is responsibility." – Winston Churchill

We've talked about leading yourself and the organization — staff and volunteers. But you have another vital role as a nonprofit leader — leading your board of directors.

Well-performing agencies all have well-performing boards. Everything begins at the top. An agency with a strong board, yet underperforming team can still reach some modest level of success. But an agency with an underperforming board but a strong team will consistently struggle to accomplish goals and achieve their mission.

Poor leadership (at the board or executive director level) will drive away good team members and board members.

Your role in leading the board is unique, in that the relationship between the executive director (or CEO) and the board is different than the leadership role you have with your staff and volunteers.

In the simplest terms, the board has one employee — you, the leader. The board's role is to govern the organization, provide leadership oversight and accountability, keep the organization true to the mission, serve as ambassadors in the community, and support the efforts of the agency as much as possible. As a member of the board, they also have a role of providing financial support to the organization.

Your role is to work with your board to ensure the agency has the best chance of achieving its mission, using the resources — people, dollars, etc. — that have been entrusted to your leadership. Your board is there to set the direction and high-level plan. They have trusted *you* to execute that plan to the best of your abilities.

It is your job to keep them informed about agency progress, the challenges you face in reaching your goals, and to leverage their knowledge, experience, and expertise to make the best decisions possible.

To be a successful *impactful* leader of a nonprofit, you must be able to lead your *whole* team — staff, volunteers, and board of directors.

What Should Your Board Be Doing?

Before you can lead your board well, you first need a clear understanding of their role and responsibilities. You need to know what an effective board (and board member) actually looks like, so you can work to create these in your own agency.

Depending on the size of the organization a board may fill many roles. In a small agency the board may provide everything from leadership to helping serve meals in the soup kitchen.

In a large organization the board may only provide high-level direction and governance — leaving the day-to-day responsibilities to the employees and volunteers.

But no matter the size of the agency, a nonprofit board has several primary responsibilities for which they are *solely* responsible.

The 8 Key Responsibilities of Nonprofit Boards

1. The board sets the vision, mission, and values of the agency and ensures they are carefully followed.

Everything the agency does is based upon its purpose, what it hopes to accomplish, and its values, or how it has determined to act, while carrying out its work. All goals, programs, budgeting, processes, and culture of how it operates emanate from the agency's mission, vision, and values. The board is responsible to set the mission, vision, and values and then ensure the agency carefully and consistently follows them.

2. They ultimately decide what is to be done, for whom, and in what manner.

Setting agency operational parameters is an important board responsibility. It's also the board's job to establish the agency's purpose, identify the client to be served, and what that service entails. While the board will undoubtedly seek guidance from others, ultimately it is their job to define the agency's scope of service and client to be served. Ultimately, the board is responsible to hire, manager and assess the CEO's performance.

3. A board is responsible for setting the culture.

This culture usually stems from the core values of the organization — guidelines about how the staff, volunteers, board members, and clients will treat each other. Typically, this involves respect for others, integrity in one's communication and carrying out one's role at the agency. Everyone is best served when there is a clear understanding of expectations throughout the entire the agency—from the mail room to the board room.

4. They protect the organization by providing oversight over agency activity and results.

Every nonprofit board's primary responsibility is to ensure that resources are used wisely, and that the agency restricts its activities to those that directly impact the mission. The agency's performance in important areas (programming, expenses, impact, etc.) should be monitored and measured. It is the board's responsibility to obtain and review those reports to ensure the agency is meeting its goals, operating effectively and efficiently.

5. They are responsible for tracking, evaluating, and reporting financial performance.

One of a board's most important responsibilities is ensuring the agency's financial sustainability and propriety. Therefore, it must closely monitor the agency's financial status. Is the agency following its own budget? Are appropriate checks and balances in place so all funds and agency assets are protected and used properly? Are all auditor comments/recommendations followed post audit?

6. They should be concerned with long term sustainability.

Boards have to think both short term and long term when setting budgets, approving new initiatives, etc. This takes dispassionate thinking, being willing to ask tough questions and sometimes make hard and unpopular decisions.

7. They should protect the agency's mission.

A board is said to "own" the agency's mission statement. One of its top responsibilities is to ensure the mission statement and its implications are clearly understood and that all decisions are made in accordance. While seemingly constrictive, closely following the mission statement makes everything much easier—budgeting, decision-making, hiring and recruiting, program development, etc.

8. They are responsible for oversight and should be ensuring everything — processes, procedures, and, activities — are performed in compliance with the controlling laws.

Every board should have a Board Policy Manual which contains all agreed upon board protocols and major decisions. There should also be written policies and procedures for agency staff and volunteers to ensure work is being done correctly, consistently, safely, and efficiently.

In the coming sections, we'll take a closer look at how these responsibilities play out in an agency, what a great board and great board member looks like, and how to operate your board for maximum impact.

CHAPTER 8

The Makings of a Great Board Director

A winning team starts with great players.

You want an incredible board — and you *need* one — if you want to take your organization further. A strong board of directors can help you get there, but it starts with a clear understanding of what makes a great player. You can't expect your team to perform well together if you don't start from the bottom up. So let's start with the basics. What does a great board director look like?

The 8 Characteristics of an *Incredible* Board Member

1. **They should demonstrate a passion for the mission.**

   There are two key points here. First, keep in mind, board service is not for someone who just finds your agency interesting. Ideally, there should be some level of commitment, even a passion, for your cause before they came to your organization. Being mildly interested or concerned may not be a deep enough commitment for candidate to fulfill the duties and responsibilities of a director.

Have they spent the last five years volunteering with organizations that help underprivileged children? Were they previously on the board for an agency working with teenagers convicted of crimes?

A passion for the cause (in general) should be apparent from their background or previous nonprofit involvement. Without this passion you may find it difficult to truly engage a board director, and more importantly — keep them around during tough times.

2. They should have a developed track record of service to your agency or another one with a similar mission.

Too often, I see agencies take on new directors who are not fully committed or don't fully understand the cause. These candidates should be given a chance to volunteer on projects, committees, or special events, to learn more.

Not only does it help a potential board member learn more about an agency, but it also gives the board a chance to see how they perform in a variety of situations and determine if they would fit in well with the board.

3. They are a strategic, disciplined, and critical thinker.

Successful boards spend a lot of time looking into the future. They consider the potential operating environment, asking themselves what needs to be done now so the agency is prepared for the future it envisions. What challenges and opportunities must the agency be prepared to handle?

A strategic thinker doesn't get lost in the details of running the agency today, unless a significant problem develops requiring some short-term focus. Good directors should be forward-focused, thinking about the big picture.

Hockey legend Wayne Gretzky was told by his father: "Skate to where the puck is going, not where it has been."

A disciplined-thinker, is a person who thinks clearly, rationally, and based on evidence. They can look at things and assess their natural consequences by following them to their logical conclusions. This type of thinking helps agencies think clearly and become successful long term, by minimizing unpleasant surprises.

Critical thinkers know how to look at a problem or challenge from multiple angles. They don't just see *what* the problem is, but they study the *why*. They are able to connect dots to create new ideas and come up with out-of-the-box solutions to problems.

Nonprofits — even more so than traditional for-profit companies — often find themselves in uniquely challenging situations. Constantly restrained by budgets, limited resources, and often overwhelming need, having critical thinkers on the board is essential for surviving these challenges.

4. They are recruited to fill a specific role. They fully embrace and perform well in that role.

Directors should be recruited — in part — based on their skills, competencies, or connections that help the agency achieve its mission.

Thinking about filling a current open spot on your board? When a list of candidates is being developed, the governance committee should consider the agency's strategic plan and determine who is missing from the board that can help the agency succeed.

There may be a need for marketing strategy or online media, or perhaps for financial expertise, or someone with access to philanthropy-minded people.

When a person with a specific talent or skill is recruited onto a board — and they *understand* the role they are asked to play — they quickly engage on the board. They know *why* they were recruited and *what* they are being asked to do.

5. They understand and follow the outlined roles and responsibilities of a director.

Many directors have little to no understanding of their role and responsibilities. It's wise to discuss the expectations for board members so they have a clear idea of how you see their role in the organization. New and even seasoned directors may be unaware of their fiduciary duties (Duty of Care, Duty of Loyalty, and Duty of Obedience).

They may not understand they will be required to serve on committees, volunteer at certain major events, support the agency financially, or how much time role and responsibilities will take.

6. They understand that a board's primary responsibility is to provide governance for the agency.

While some small and start up boards have an active role in day-to-day operations, most boards should not. The board should stick to managing their "sole employee" — the executive director.

7. They understand the governance vs. volunteer vs. participant roles they may play.

A board member can only act in a governance role while acting in the capacity of being a member of the board. If a director is volunteering as a greeter in church or handing out food in a food pantry, during that time they are only volunteers and cannot (and should not) act in their capacity of a board member.

8. They should have a bias toward action, be engaged, proactive, and always prepared.

A high value board candidate becomes a board member because he or she wants to accomplish things that help the agency. They will be active, want to see progress and results, and always be prepared for meetings. They won't stick around if the board meetings are boring, unproductive, or a waste of time.

A proactive on-boarding process can help get new directors up to speed quickly and engaged fast. If they sit around for three to six months without saying or doing anything, you may lose them to another organization.

What Else Should You Know?

If you're in the process of recruiting board members, let me share with you a common error many nonprofits make. It's easy to do, but I want you to be the leader that doesn't do it. It might be quick and easy in the short-term, but you'll pay for it later.

Don't settle for just any candidate because you have an opening.

Let me repeat. Please don't settle for your neighbor's friend's brother who happens to think saving one-legged monkeys is a great cause. You barely know anything about him. He definitely doesn't know anything about you. Just because he's interested — *and available* — doesn't mean he'll help make your board (or organization) better.

Just like that awkward first date you had with your roommate's cousin your freshman year in college…

If the fit isn't good up front, it won't get any better later. You'll have wasted an opening on the board on someone who adds no value. You're much better off keeping the spot open until you find a candidate you really want.

Good volunteers do not automatically make good board members.

An outstanding volunteer uses specific skills in their role — skills that may not translate to a role on the board of directors. Great volunteer service alone is not a valid reason to invite a volunteer onto the board.

Jane runs the annual golf outing flawlessly. Months of planning, dozens of volunteers, and she's got a heck of a swing too. Each year she does an incredible job with your event, hobnobbing with all the bigwigs, inspiring the volunteers, and raising a large amount of donations. You love Jane. The people that come to the event love Jane. She's awesome. That doesn't necessarily make her a good candidate for the board.

While running an outing requires strong leadership and management skills, a board role requires shared leadership, collaboration, thoughtful discussions, strategic thinking, and reflection. It involves making decisions as a team and being hands-off when those decisions turn into actionable tasks.

Don't get me wrong. Jane might be incredible on your board, but don't be quick to put her in that role by default, just because it's open.

My suggestion? Ask Jane to serve on 1-2 board committees as a non-director member and see how well she works out in a collaborative atmosphere. If she excels, you may have your next director. If it's not a good fit, both she and you will know, and will avoid a lot of heartache and frustration later.

Always be on the look-out for your next board candidates, every day, all year long.

If you want an outstanding board, you need outstanding candidates. Unless you're incredibly lucky, those outstanding candidates aren't lined up outside your door just waiting for you, and they generally don't fall in your lap.

Keep a running list of the people you meet that you think might make incredible board members. Work to get to know them better. Try to get them involved in your organization in some way to see how they do. As you get to know them better, push them up or down in priority on your list. When a spot opens up, you will already have someone in mind.

Watch for great players (from other teams).

If someone is currently on another board and unable to join yours right now, be sure to reach out to them every so often so they know you're still interested. Send updates from your organization, meet for coffee, or invite them to an event you're having. Just because they aren't available now, doesn't mean they won't be a good fit later. They key is to stay in touch so when they're available, you're ready.

Look beyond your friends and family members, no matter how tempted you may be to add them.

I know your sister-in-law is incredible and she's so outgoing and personable that she just has to be a good fit on the board.

You're sure she could help fundraise and sell the organization and you really need to fill that spot that opened up…

While it's not *always* a bad idea, adding close friends and family members to the board can create issues. Not only can it be difficult to have any potentially negative conversations in the future, but others on the board may see it as a form of favoritism or a way to push your own agenda through the board.

Don't recruit a lot of like-minded or similar-thinking people.

You want diversity of thought on your board. Having a room full of yes-people almost ensures the agency will fail. Your critical governance role will be weak, and your creative thinking will be limited at best. To succeed you need the best people in the room sharing their best thinking.

Having a little creative friction on the board is a good thing. Of course, with diversity of thought, there will be disagreements. But as long as you have a culture of mutual respect, and directors are focusing on what is best for the agency you should be able to work through these challenges and reach common ground.

Major donors don't *automatically* make good directors.

I wish I hadn't lived through this, again and again on various boards. I've seen many examples of a major donor believing he or she can exert certain pressure on board decisions by virtue of their financial support.

I know of one social service agency that turned down a request to join the board by an annual six-figure donor. The board felt those future checks would come with expectations, baggage, and unnecessary pressure that wouldn't be healthy for the agency.

It took guts, but in their situation, it was the right thing to do. The potential negative impact to the agency outweighed the positive impact that would have been made by the donation.

And my last words of wisdom on what makes a good board member…

Effective board members are not afraid to speak the truth as they understand it.

You want board members who will step up and tell you how they see things. It takes moral courage and character to disagree with a leader — and especially, to challenge something that just doesn't seem right. It can also make for unpleasant discussions. But if everyone speaks their mind (respectfully) in truth and is trusted as not having a hidden agenda, the board benefits greatly from such transparency.

CHAPTER 9

From Great Players to an Incredible Team

It takes more than great directors to build a great board.

In his best-selling book *Good to Great* Jim Collins said:

"Get the right people on the bus, the wrong people off the bus, and the right people in the right seats on the bus."

His point was simple. Without the right team, in the right place, you will struggle to succeed. I believe this is no less true for nonprofit boards than it is within for-profit leadership.

A struggling board may be the single, most significant reason nonprofit agencies of all types and sizes fail to reach their highest potential, or worse, close their doors.

When a board doesn't do its job effectively, either due to a lack of training or weak governance practices, the agency is at risk.

When there is no oversight of leadership, no questioning of leadership or accountability, no oversight of mission, values, strategic plan, or programming, the agency becomes vulnerable to poor performance and indifference.

I've worked with a number of nonprofits and often the board concerns from well-meaning executive directors and board chairs are the same.

- Directors don't come to meetings prepared.
- They don't understand their role.
- They don't share their thoughts when asked.
- They don't ask any questions.
- They aren't engaged in the organization.
- They leave after board meetings and go silent.

Do any of these things sound familiar in your agency?

A well-intended but weak or untrained board can lead to mission creep, ineffective operations, failing client services, and even the ultimate demise of an organization.

But a well-built board — consisting of passionate people with varying skills and experiences — helps the organization focus on its mission. Since there are no hidden agendas, everyone knows where the organization is headed and how it intends to get there.

Mutual trust and respect are the secret sauce that will elevate the board's performance and ripple throughout the entire organization.

This culture is also an extremely attractive feature when you are recruiting new directors, new employees, and new volunteers.

A high value board will insist on clarity of mission, tight alignment of resources, and a laser focus on the activities the *most* impact the mission. Their guidance and support help the CEO keep the most important thing, the most important thing.

A high-functioning board will lead to higher agency performance. The board's energy, focus, passion, and commitment to excellence will lead to improved results. This is often one of the key things reviewed by donors and/or funders. They will always ask, "What difference are you making *today* with the funds you have, and how will *our funding* help you *increase or sustain* those results?"

Will you be ready and able to answer that question well?

How do you go about building an *effective,* high-functioning board of directors?

Fortunately, we can look to successful boards for clues and identify certain standards, best practices, and characteristics they all seem to have. You can then work to bring about these characteristics in your own board.

I believe there are 20 key characteristics of good boards. I know it seems like a daunting list, but as you review these 20 elements please keep this in mind — building an effective board should be seen as a journey.

If you spend time intentionally working on your board, you will see positive results with even incremental progress.

The next section offers a high-level overview of the 19 characteristics. The rest of the chapter will be devoted to expanding on each of these characteristics so you can learn more about how they could work in your organization.

As you read through the list, I invite you to pause on each of these and think about whether or not you notice these in your agency. If you find your board is missing many of these elements, don't worry — you are right in line with most other agencies. If you choose even 3-5 of these characteristics and work towards improving your board, you will see quickly see dramatic results.

The 20 Characteristics of an *effective* board.

1. They know how to build and sustain themselves.
2. They don't just happen. Effective boards are the product of ongoing training, self-assessment, you have to work at maintaining and elevating their performance.
3. They understand their three legal responsibilities.
4. They create, manage, and track Strategic Plan progress.
5. They ensure financial integrity and agency sustainability.
6. They understand each role of the board, the unique

differences, and which one(s) they are to fulfill.

7. They are strategic in their recruiting.
8. They have comprehensive orientation and training programs for new board members and conduct periodic refresher training for existing members.
9. They know the fundraising strengths of each director and use them accordingly. They clearly articulate the board's role in fundraising.
10. They measure and evaluate program *and* financial results.
11. They create, maintain, and follow a Board Policy Manual.
12. They enforce their own term limits provisions.
13. They know they have *one* employee to manage-the executive director and hold them accountable for results.
14. They understand they must set clear boundaries between board and staff roles.
15. They strive to run effective meetings.
16. They have *and follow* a Risk Management Program.
17. They conduct periodic organizational assessments and annual board evaluations for operations, strategy, structure, and operational effectiveness.
18. They have open and honest communication.
19. Effective boards celebrate and reward successes.
20. They take time for reflection/ discussion about the agency. and its operating environment.

How many of these characteristics do you think your board already has? If it's more than half I applaud your efforts. Many boards will struggle to successfully embody even a few of the 20 elements. But hope is not lost. There are many things you can do to start improving your board. Let's start by taking a bit of time to explore each of these characteristics.

The 20 Characteristics of an *Effective* Board — and what they really look like.

1. Effective boards know how to build (and sustain) themselves.

Your board of directors needs to have a solid understanding of what an effective board looks like, how it should conduct itself, and most importantly, their role and responsibilities within the organization. They should also know what it takes to make the board better and what is required to maintain this level of effectiveness.

You may want to share the list of the 20 key characteristics — or this entire chapter — with your board, or at least the board chair. Many board members don't even realize there are specific characteristics needed to be effective.

2. Effective boards don't just happen; it takes consistent attention to the little things to maintain a high level of effectiveness.

Coming to meetings prepared, completing all commitments, showing up for meetings and functions, and offering straight talk all goes in to being effective.

Just like donations, you have to be intentional about building and sustaining an effective board. Your board members should recognize that it takes effort to build (and maintain) a high-functioning team. It takes work to keep everyone on the same page, communicating effectively, and working as a team to achieve agency goals. The board chair and chair of the governance Committee play key roles keeping the board perform at a high value level.

3. They understand their three legal responsibilities as a board.

While boards in various size nonprofits may have any number of responsibilities, it's important to understand there are 3 specific *legal* responsibilities a board has to a nonprofit organization. If your board is struggling and you want to better define roles and responsibilities, you will want to start here.

Duty of Care

A board member owes the duty to exercise reasonable care when making decisions as a steward of the agency. This duty is often explained as the care that a reasonably prudent director would exercise in a similar position and under similar situations.

Directors must consider the consequences of their decisions and act reasonably in their role as decision-maker and influencer because an agency is a legal entity and directors are elected to protect it and administer it correctly. The donating public is counting on that.

For instance, when negotiating contracts for the agency, the board should obtain the same kind of contact terms it would want if the directors were negotiating the terms for themselves personally. All spending decisions should be made responsibly, as if they were spending their own money. When carrying out their board duties, their job is to act in a prudent manner, protecting the agency's interests.

Duty of Loyalty

A board member must provide undivided allegiance when making decisions affecting the agency. Their duty in this capacity is to represent the agency *only* and act in its best interests. Any real or potential conflicts of interest must be disclosed to the rest of the board so it can decide if the director must recuse himself or take special steps instead to ensure transparency and that the agency is fairly treated.

For example, a director's full-time job may be in a business that the agency uses, like accounting or printing services. That director's firm might be able to contract with the agency to provide services, but the potential conflict must be identified and declared to the board. The board member should not be benefitting unfairly from their role on the board.

These types of situations can get sticky, so most agencies avoid them altogether if possible. If you must go down this road, full disclosure is best. If you have to hide anything from other members of your board, you're already at risk.

Duty of Obedience

Board members must remain faithful to the agency's mission, abide by all laws and regulations, and not participate in any illegal activities. They are not permitted to act in any way that is inconsistent with the mission, central goals of the agency, or outside its legal and financial boundaries.

They also must understand that they cannot act unilaterally on behalf of the agency, even though they are a director. This can be very tempting when out in public, or when representing the agency at an event, but it is strictly outside the bounds of being a director. A director's power and influence resides in their membership of the entire board.

The public trusts that the leaders of the agency will manage donated funds and conduct themselves in a way to fulfills the agency's stated mission.

For example, if the agency's activities began to drift away from its mission and away from what donors felt they were supporting, the board would need to step in and take steps to ensure the agency stayed true to its mission.

Another example would be if the agency began using questionable accounting measures to improve its outlook. This would be a violation of the Duty of Obedience.

4. An effective board creates, manages, and monitors progress on its strategic plan.

All boards — regardless of nonprofit size — are tasked with the responsibility to approve their agency's strategic plan. But the creation, management, and execution of the plan may differ by organization. There's no right or wrong to go about it, as long as the plan itself has had the "green light" by the board.

Some plans are created and approved by the board and then given to the CEO (Executive Director) for implementation. Others are created by a group composed of the board and members of the agency's leadership team. In a few cases, it is created solely by the leadership team and simply approved by the board. By far, the most frequent method is a combination of board members and the leadership team.

A complete plan includes the agency's vision, mission, values, key strategies and major goals. These documents set a clear expectation throughout the agency of where it is going and how it intends to get there.

These documents provide the high-level guidance for virtual every decision the agency makes. If some activity, program, or initiative is not covered by, or in line with the plan — or does not further the agency's mission — it should be avoided.

The same applies to budgets. Only expenses that directly relate to the mission, as detailed in the strategic plan, should be included.

Many agencies have a track record of permitting mission creep. That is, going beyond its initial purpose and doing other things, arguably beyond its mission. This starts out with very small, incremental steps but can take an agency far off course, not to mention far from where its donors expected it to go.

If your mission was to help feed the homeless, then you shouldn't be trying to offer housing as well, unless it was part of your strategic plan. If you want to make it part of your strategic plan — and expand the mission of the organization — this needs to be something the board approves.

It can be easy to see a jump like this as not being part of the plan, but the slippery slope starts when a client you're serving asks if they can stay in your organization for a few hours longer after eating, because it's snowing outside. A decision you make in the moment to provide for those you serve, can quickly create mission creep, pushing your facilities and team potentially past what they can offer. It may also be creating risk you aren't yet prepared to manage.

Smart leaders use their plan to create agendas for their staff meetings and effective boards use them to establish agendas for their board and committee meetings. This practice ensures the agency stays on mission and accomplishes what it previously determined was critical to its mission.

If you're concerned about mission creep, list the services you are currently offering. Ask yourself which of these might not be closely aligned with the original mission. Present the list at the next board meeting and get input and feedback. You may find that your team is burning out because you're just doing too much.

Without a plan, an agency has no direction and cannot accomplish very much. It may have many hard-working individuals, but they may be wasting a lot of time and resources through uncertainty, making missteps, recruiting the wrong people, or not focusing on the most important things.

Effective agencies ensure all resources and efforts are aligned with the mission. If something doesn't fit, it's tabled for possible future versions of the plan.

One of the most critical way boards operate successfully is by viewing everything through the filter of the strategic plan. All board decisions, budget allocations, and priorities are set by ensuring they are in line with the agency's mission, vision, values, and strategic plan.

Sometime in the last year or so, your board and key staff likely established several strategic goals at a retreat. Until they are changed or revised by the board, your decisions and actions should work towards achieving those objectives.

When a board reviews a budget proposal, or a proposed set of priorities for the coming year, or decides whether to investigate new opportunities it sees, it should do so in light of its mission, vision, values, and strategic plan. Yes or no decisions become clearer and easier to make when the board uses those guidelines as hard and fast rules.

Unless there are clear and overwhelming reasons for a board to disregard or deviate from its well-crafted and well-thought out plan, it should stick with it.

5. An effective board ensures financial integrity and agency sustainability.

The saying goes "no money, no mission" and no truer words have been spoken.

Perhaps a board's most sensitive responsibility is how it receives, manages — and *spends* — the funds donated to the agency. Board members are fiduciaries, meaning directors hold positions of great public trust. With that comes certain legal responsibilities. Board members are called to be good stewards of the resources provided. These duties require careful scrutiny of expenditures and care when preparing budgets.

Boards should ideally review agency financial reports each month, but at minimum each quarter, with a few key questions in mind.

How many sources of revenue does the agency have, and what are they? Are they reliable so can they be counted in the future? Is the agency relying on too few sources to fund its work? Are expenses in line with the budget and mission?

These questions help in managing not only today's revenue but help the agency plan for success in the future. The board is a caretaker of the agency and its duties include protecting it for the long term.

6. Effective boards understand each role they can play in the agency, the unique differences, and which one(s) they are charged to fulfill.

The board may act in up to three roles in their service to the agency. These roles are *governance*, *strategic*, and *operational* (working). Let's look a bit closer at each of these roles.

Every board has a *governance* role, meaning they are responsible to create, establish, and monitor all processes and policies of the agency. This is a significant responsibility and often -- when an agency experiences significant problems -- it is due to a breakdown in governance.

In the role of governance, the board is responsible to ensure all legal requirements and self-imposed rules and policies are followed.

The second of the 3 key roles is the *strategic* role. All boards have a duty to periodically look into the future and ensure the agency is positioning itself to succeed both now -- and in the future, when operating conditions may be significantly different.

In today's increasingly dynamic world, anticipating the future — while very challenging — is an absolute must if you want your agency to survive. If your board does not try to anticipate the changes your organization may encounter, you run the risk of shrinking, failing, or becoming obsolete and insignificant.

The *operational* or *working* role is usually filled by the boards of new or very small agencies. This is a board that rolls up its sleeves and does much of the administrative and volunteer work. They not only monitor processes and policies, but also perform many of the necessary work so the agency can operate.

Think stuffing envelopes, picking out the color of napkins for the gala, making deposits at the bank, preparing checks to pay bills, going out to obtain auction items for the annual dinner fundraiser event, or serving food in the kitchen.

There is nothing wrong with a board performing these additional duties as long as it still performs its other two (primary) duties as well. The key is to understand that a board must first provide governance and strategic oversight. Only *then* can it help operate.

7. Effective boards are strategic in how they identify and recruit new candidates.

In the same way that you are thoughtful and strategic about how you hire employees for your team, your board should use the same care and attention when recruiting new potential board members.

They should begin reviewing the strategic plan to identify any specific skills or capabilities that would be helpful to have in a new director. This is a chance to align the future direction of the agency with board members who have some skill, some network, some resources that will greatly help the agency achieve its goals.

For example, let's say your organization plans to expand and build their own building in the next 1-3 years. You may want to look to someone that has construction experience, or at least knows the industry. They may be able to offer insight to prevent or solve future challenges.

Your board should maintain an ongoing confidential list of board candidates so top candidates can be identified and approached ahead of time at opportune moments as openings occur.

I've seen so many agencies wait until 60 or even 30 days before an opening to start thinking about a replacement. I can't tell you how many times I've been on a board and heard, "Does anyone know of someone who might want to serve on our board"?

This *shotgun* approach doesn't do your agency, board, or the potential candidate any favors. While you should *definitely* ask for suggestions from your current board members for new potential members — they can be a wonderful source of referrals — relying on this to fill essential board positions can leave you high and dry and scrambling for talent at the last minute.

Once you've identified a potential board member, I recommend inviting them to serve on a board committee first, before offering them a seat on the board. This experience can help you see how they work with other directors and learn if they would be a good cultural fit for the board. Only then should you decide whether to invite the candidate to apply for the open seat.

It's much easier to simply *not invite* a committee member to continue to serve then it is to oust a board member that isn't performing or working well with your board.

8. Effective nonprofit boards have comprehensive orientation and training programs for new board members.

They also conduct refresher training for existing members.

New board members typically begin their board service with very little understanding of their duties, responsibilities, and what is expected of them. They will often sit quietly in board meetings for the first 3-6 months of their term. They listen carefully, but are often reluctant to say something, afraid of sounding uninformed or stupid. This is a terrible waste of talent and new ideas.

But you can supercharge new directors and begin to benefit from their presence immediately if you take the time to train them on your procedures and share with them the key issues the agency is currently facing. There may be a role the new director can play right away.

Once you've identified, vetted, and recruited your new board member, it's essential to provide orientation and training so they can get up to speed quickly, feel involved, and start contributing.

Effective boards take the time to explain what they expect from the new director. Each director — *in theory* — has been recruited for specific reasons and it's helpful to let them know how they can best serve the board and the agency. Some directors are recruited for their financial, marketing or previous leadership skills, others for access to their network.

Clarifying a director's role on the board has many benefits. Not only does the new director know why he or she is there and what they are supposed to do, but it also gives them a sense of purpose, responsibility, and belonging.

Keep in mind — a board with new directors needs time to become a cohesive team. By providing upfront training and then assigning a director to a committee, or to get involved in a specific initiative, they will become quickly immersed in key issues, and feel part of the team much faster. We will talk more in detail about developing a board training and orientation program later.

9. Effective boards know the fundraising strengths of each director and use them accordingly. They clearly articulate the board's role in fundraising.

Too often, candidates are recruited onto a board without being told of the "give or get" requirement. Sometimes, financial support for an agency is one of those very personal and potentially "charged" topics — especially if the newly minted board member had no previous knowledge of that obligation.

Since this topic (or its required level of support) can sometimes be a most unpleasant surprise — if not a straight up deal killer — it is far better to get this topic on the table early on in your board recruitment process. Mishandling this topic can cause negative feelings, could result in the director in question losing some enthusiasm for the agency, or worst case, influence them to leave the board and agency altogether.

Effective boards ensure each board member knows they have a responsibility to donate and raise funds — or at least help. They should also know that many funders (foundations, grantors, etc.) ask how much the directors themselves give. So, like it or not, they are all in development in some way.

Some directors are much better at it than others. Some fully embrace the responsibility and excel, others can't imagine asking someone for money. But even directors who resist asking for donations can play helpful and important roles in the agency's fundraising efforts.

The key is to know your board members and their abilities. Don't ask someone to do what they are uncomfortable doing. Neither of you will be happy with the results. The same holds true for fundraising. Use people's greatest strengths in fundraising where they can thrive.

Think about any successful sports team manager or head coach. They will tell you they try to put their individual players in a position where they can be successful. If the team needs a base hit, a batter on the bench with a high hitting average will be called upon to pinch bat. If a basketball team needs a three-point play at the end to win, the coach will send his best three-point shooters onto the court. The same holds true for board members and fundraising.

There are many roles a director can play other than asking friends for money. They can write thank you notes or make calls. They can develop the script others will use when meeting donors. They can deliver (or co-present) short talks at community service group meetings like the Rotary, Chamber of Commerce, etc. They can join with others to visit a potential donor or to thank long-time supporter. They could even host a reception at a golf course or elsewhere so others can be invited to learn about the agency.

Periodic training to help board members can also polish one's fundraising skills. A board can provide training from a specialist to help directors develop their approach, style and comfort in asking for support. There is a basic tactical approach to fundraising, and you may find most directors just need a little help development (and getting comfortable with) their "pitch" or elevator speech.

You can try having some fun with this by engaging in role play and then reviewing each practice attempt.

If you get complaints from your directors about fundraising, remind them gently that fundraising is an expectation of board service and critical to the success of the organization.

I'll end this topic of board fundraising with a quick story.

I once met an individual who told me his board only met three times a year, for two days. On the first morning of each meeting they go around the table and each director has to explain how much money he or she had raised since their last meeting. If that's not transparency, I don't know what is…

10. Effective boards measure and evaluate both program and financial results.

Best-selling author Peter Drucker once said, "'What gets measured, gets improved." This is no less true for boards.

Some people don't like measuring results, especially when they are in the "business" of serving others. But metrics serve a very important purpose—they help us get and *stay* on course towards our goals. They can be the magnet as it were, pulling us back to true north if we begin to deviate from the path towards our goals.

How will you know if you are fulfilling your mission unless you track progress and results? How else can you assure donors your agency is worthy of their investment?

The secret is to pick the right things to measure. What are the right things? Whatever key metrics will help you tell your story and demonstrate your success.

Many use *input metrics*. For instance, churches use attendance, donations, square footage, programs, baptisms, or the number of regional church plants to measure impact. Social service agencies may use the number of people they have fed, clothed, housed, or even the amount of clothing given away. These are nice but don't tell the real story of how effective you are in your mission.

I believe the best metrics (aside from your critical financial performance metrics) are the *output metrics*. These include the number of people gaining employment, or permanent housing. If the mission of your agency is to end homelessness, and you only track the number of people you feed each day, it really doesn't convey progress towards your mission. But reporting that last year you helped 63 people off the streets and into permanent homes, will go a long way to showing progress. You can even measure your own progress against previous years.

From a financial standpoint it's a little easier to track results. It's important to pay close attention to cash flow, revenue, and expenses. Factors like the number of separate revenue streams, how reliable they are, and recent trends, can help you create realistic budgets that are achievable.

Remember, it's not enough to just measure or review metrics. An effective board will use these metrics to make critical decisions about the agency moving forward.

11. Effective boards create, maintain, and follow their own Board Policy Manual.

I know… I just used the words Policy Manual, and you're looking around for something to save you.

Don't fade out on me now. While the title is… less than scintillating… this manual is one of the very best tools an agency can use to become "best in class" or even just as a set of ground rules to keep improving.

Now here's the good with the bad. While it is your own personal manual, uniquely created with you in mind, the downside is, you have to create it yourself.

One of the most common mistakes every nonprofit makes, is not following its own rules, processes, and procedures. Making a habit of this can lead to a number of problems — some of them quite serious.

A Board Policy Manual is a living (changing) document that contains copies of every board decision that has to do with policy, processes, procedures. They can include:

- The bylaws
- Position descriptions
- Strategic plan
- Goals
- Conflict of Interest Policy
- Investment Policy
- Gift Policy
- Financial Controls Policy
- Whistle Blower Policy
- Document Retention Policy
- Risk management Policy

And many others…

If you keep a copy of important board decisions handy, you'll be consistent in your decision-making when similar issues arise. Agencies get in trouble with inconsistency of issue handling. This can open the door to problems — some of them legal and/or very expensive to make go away.

12. An effective board enforces its term limits provisions.

Every good thing must come to an end. Every board needs to manage its director turnover to remain healthy, vibrant, and aware of its changing operating environment. Boards with no term limits provision — or those that ignore the limits set — typically end up with an embedded group of directors who usually just maintain the status quo.

Newton's 1st law? *An object at rest stays at rest… until someone kicks it in the pants.* Okay, so I took a few liberties on that one, but I'm pretty sure that's what he meant…

A group of people that have been "together forever" are going to keep things "like they've always been". Without new people on the board there will be little to no new ideas and new opportunities will rarely have a chance to be heard or tested.

In the worst cases I've seen long serving directors forget just who owns that agency and remember it's not them. Those directors begin thinking in terms of it being *their* agency. This can change the way they think and act in their roles. They forget they aren't the owners but only there to *take care* of the agency.

Fresh thinking, new ideas, new board dynamics all keeps a board healthy and at the top of its game.

Successful boards avoid having to many long-time, or too many new board members on at any one time. Ideally, there should be a continuous supply of candidates who can serve and take the place of those whose time has come to steps aside.

I once served on a social service board dominated by long-time serving directors who just would not be open to new ideas or ways of doing things. Needless to say, I did not stay around very long. In fact, I probably did a poor job of evaluating that board before I ever joined it.

On another board, I fought hard (successfully, eventually) to reinstall its own term limits that it had voted into suspension mode to better launch a $2.5mm major gift campaign. I did get the term limit provision reactivated, but it did not feel like a "win".

I guarantee if any of those directors had a small picture of me in their wallets or purses, at least a few of them discarded it along the way. Still, it was the right thing to do. You can avoid all this drama by following your term limits provisions.

Another challenge with long-time embedded directors is that they can stifle the development of your newer directors by expressly or inadvertently quashing their new ideas and cautioning them on why their ideas won't work in your agency. Phrases like "we tried that once" or "we don't do it that way around here" will discourage a newer director and could result in their stepping off of the board altogether. Once word gets around, you'll have a harder time recruiting high value candidates the next time.

Letting someone step down for a year — even a high value board member — is healthy for both the director and the board. It gives both parties a chance to step back and refresh themselves. You can always consider adding them back in a year.

A little "house cleaning" also frees up the board to do some new thinking about issues so it can make decisions that are best for the agency, and not just best for the one person that was a strong advocate.

One agency I knew waved its term limits provision so it could keep its board intact during a $3 million campaign. Well, 7-8 years later, it still was ignoring its bylaws which clearly called for 2 to 3-year terms for directors. While they raised the money, the agency had no pipeline of new directors to systematically step onto the board.

Eventually they began following their bylaws but imagine the turmoil as half their board (8 members) exited at the same time, and an influx of new directors stepped in fairly quickly. That is just too much historical knowledge and experience walking off of the board at one time.

If they had enforced their term limits and pushed directors to leave during their campaign do you really think those that would have left wouldn't have helped out anyway, even if they had stepped down? I am sure they would have worked just as hard to raise the money, whether they were still directors, or not.

If you don't have term limits in your bylaws or if you don't observe them, I encourage you to figure out how to make them a part of your culture and standard procedure again. Not only do term limits allow for a fresh new perspective, but a hidden benefit can be that they can help you remove a difficult board member. It can be tempting to "stick with what works" but remember, you never know what might work even better...

13. An effective board knows it has one employee to manage — the executive director and holds him or her accountable for results.

Boards get in trouble when they forget they are directors, not CEO's. When boards overstep their governance role and begin managing staff, telling them what to do, how to do it, etc., they've gone too far.

This can happen innocently enough when board members serve on a committee which is led by a staff member — like a gala or a fund development committee. In those cases, directors are acting only in their capacity as volunteers, not as directors. When directors forget to honor the line between director and volunteer, they can cause chaos, bad feelings, and disunity.

It is the board's job to monitor the agency's progress on its goals and to hold the executive director accountable for results. Too often, the board abdicates this responsibility and doesn't conduct an annual review or provide any meaningful feedback to the executive director.

This breakdown leads to poor communication and sometimes — issues. When people hold back their valid concerns, opinions and expectations, these unvoiced thoughts may lead to friction and misunderstandings between the two parties.

Both the board and the executive director must demonstrate the moral courage to speak truth to each other while still maintaining mutual respect. This clarity proves that everyone is on the same side and focused on the same goals.

14. They understand they must set clear boundaries between board and staff roles.

This crossover can happen quite innocently, especially when directors and staff sit on the same staff-led committee — say a gala planning committee. To often, a well-meaning director will issue instructions to a staff member and try to manage them. This is understandable — as the board member sees themselves in a position of authority — but in a case like this, it is completely unacceptable. In a situation like this, the board member is acting in a role of a volunteer and the staff member should be leading.

15. An effective board runs effective board and committee meetings.

This may be the biggest reason high value directors step off of a board and why high value candidates never sign up. They detest meetings, especially those that waste time.

Many board members work full time. The last thing they want to do is show up for an evening/weekend meeting on their personal time where nothing meaningful takes place.

I remember one board meeting I attended on a snowy Monday night. Scheduled for 7pm - 10pm I can only tell you how much I was looking forward to an evening of discussing important things — like the color of the napkins for the annual gala...

An hour into the meeting everyone on my side of the table was looking out the window watching the weather get worse and worse, wondering if we'd get home that night... But — by some miracle — we settled on dusty mauve for the napkins. Crisis. Averted.

Your board members are committed to your mission. They're usually people of action, people who want to make things happen and make a difference. When they are forced to sit through discussions better left to a committee, or not challenged they get antsy.

A board that serves best is one that monitors current progress and looks to the future. You will get the very best from your board when you present them with reports they can understand and future focused topics to consider.

Committees are where the heavy lifting happens if more work is needed — not at the board meeting at 9pm on a snowy night...

High value board members are always on another agency's target list so if you continually bore them with little details, missing the opportunity to tap into their skill sets and interests, you run the real risk of losing them.

I stepped down from one board early because all we did was hold feel good meetings. It was boring and a waste of time. Nothing was ever accomplished. I sat on another *advisory* council, and we never got the chance to really advise, just listen. In both cases, the leaders felt they knew better and were just looking for us to rubber stamp their plans.

The directors you want on your board are busy, focused, and want to help. They want to make a difference. To ensure their complete attention and cooperation, here's a few ways to improve your board meetings.

- Send out all materials one week before the meeting.
- Keep the agenda high level, and avoid things a committee, or the staff, should handle.
- Do not allow anyone to drone on, giving a speech. No monologues. If absolutely necessary for them to speak, ask them to summarize their points briefly.
- Once a point has been made, the chair should not allow each director to repeat points already made.

When complex topics come before the board, assign them to a committee for detailed study and investigation. When the committee is ready, have them present the issue and all sides to the entire board for a discussion and vote. Resist having the entire board tackle an issue until the committee has thoroughly studied it and made its recommendations.

If you make your board sit through the health insurance benefit spread sheet analysis each year, you'll end up with no directors. Keep your meetings as brief as possible, focused on only high-level topics and key decisions. This will help keep directors awake, engaged, and coming back the next time.

16. Every agency should have (and follow) a Risk Management Program.

Ok, not quite as bad as Board Policy Manual, but it's up there. No one wants to think about a Risk Management Program — except, when things get risky….

Let's face it, bad things happen. While you can try and prevent as many as possible, you need to be prepared for worst-case. Starting to think about how to resolve a problem once it's already happened puts you under the gun — often in a very public atmosphere — and may result in you making an unwise, emotional decision.

So which risks do you need to think about? Does your agency sign contracts with others, rent space, invite the public into your offices, have a children's program, use vehicles or trucks to deliver services, collect and maintain people's personal information, or have coolers or freezers for food storage?

All of these types of situations can expose you to risk. If the answer is yes, or if you have similar situations in your organization, you need to review your processes for how to handle problems when they arise.

You should have a written policy manual outlining steps to be taken in case something occurs. Here are a few things I've seen in other agencies.

- An Emergency Succession Plan in case your leader becomes ill/ injured for a period of time.
- A Gift Acceptance Policy
- A Conflict of Interest Policy
- A Records Retention Policy
- A Personal Manual

We will go more into detail — *I know you can't wait* — on creating a Risk Management Program later. For now, it's important to know that an effective board takes steps to mitigate risk when possible.

17. Effective boards conduct periodic organizational assessments and annual board evaluations in the areas of operations, strategy, structure, and operational effectiveness.

Feedback is the critical step to excellence. Without it, you're only guessing how well your board and agency are doing. It's easy for a leader to see only what he or she wants to see and ignore the rest. It might be subconscious or unintentional, but that makes it no less real. To achieve success, a leader and board need to have accurate, unbiased feedback on a regular basis.

Organizational assessments serve as effective tools to measure the performance of the board and individual directors. They can be used to convince others that change is needed. They can also tell you how aligned your team's thinking is, help you move from compromise to consensus with decisions, and help to determine priorities.

The challenge with feedback is that people generally assume it will be negative — used to catch someone doing something wrong, rather than as a tool to help improve performance.

In her book *Prove It! How to Create a Higher Performance Culture and Measure it,* author Stacey Barr said this:

"Measuring performance is like gravity. It pulls our attention and action toward a center, toward the most important things we should focus on and improve. When we measure the important performance results, we move more directly toward those results and we achieve them sooner and with less effort.

...performance measurement... speeds up and takes effort out of our pursuit of what we want. So we get bigger and better improvements for less effort.

Evidence-based leaders can prove how well their organization is delivering what matters most — measurably and objectively and convincingly."

How successful boards measure and assess is generally a role of the governance committee. They can measure progress in several ways including:

- Conduct executive sessions (with and then without the Executive director) at the end of each board meeting and asking, "How are we doing?"

- Evaluate each director every 1-2 years with surveys.
- Use an outside evaluator who has proven assessment tools to help analyze performance and any breakdowns, when possible.
- Provide training modules on board best practices.

An effective board knows that it needs to measure and manage not only results, but progress towards and away from goals. They realize that feedback is critical and work to provide both positive and critical feedback when needed.

18. Successful boards have open communication.

They understand the benefits of showing moral courage by speaking truth, even when it may not be popular to do so. Once directors, or other leaders start bending the truth, overlooking bad behavior, or allowing the agency's values to become corrupted, the agency begins the fast and damaging trip down a slippery slope to being compromised. This is one of the reasons why good governance is so important.

Directors are not there to "play" board—they want to "be" a board. The unwritten understanding is that they have given each other permission to engage in honest straight talk, to speak their minds gracefully, with respect, and to never attack the person, just the issues or points being made.

An effective board doesn't let things fester; they keep short accounts with each other on things and bring up issues when they are small and can easily be addressed.

Don't allow your board to hold secret meetings after the meetings or talk behind someone's back. Directors should speak directly and respectfully to each other — even if the topic is unpleasant. Don't be reluctant to remind your board of the values you have adopted and that they apply to directors as well as well as staff.

19. Effective boards celebrate and reward successes.

If you want to see more of something, reward that behavior. Sadly, boards and leaders in general, are often quick with their reprimands but slow on rewarding desired behavior — if they do it at all. An effective board understands the need to recognize and celebrate the wins.

When an agency achieves a major goal or one that proved much more difficult than anticipated, why not take time to thank and recognize those who made it happen? Think how motivating a simple, unexpected thank you and some recognition can be.

While it's part of your job as a leader to recognize and celebrate the successes of your employees, an effective board knows it's their job to create a culture that promotes the same. Whether it's a successful gala, or the golf event that was rained out half-way through and moved to the clubhouse. When your team works hard towards a goal it's critical to recognize not only a win, but progress made in pursuit of that goal. These celebrations not only help morale and create a culture that attracts more great people, it also inspires more action towards the end result.

20. They take time for unstructured reflection and discussion about the agency and its operating environment.

Effective boards provide time on the agenda for unstructured, open discussion allowing directors the opportunity to generate new ideas, ask questions, reflect on the external environment, and think about how best to position the agency so it is ready for the future.

We've spent a lot of time covering the characteristics of an effective board. By now you should have an idea of how your board looks — at least on the surface. Were you able to identify things that your current board does well? Did you spot areas that might be causing issues you hadn't seen yet?

I invite you to share these characteristics with your board chair. Review the list and collect his or her feedback and input. Do each of you have unique perspectives? If you're ready, go over the high-level list at your next board meeting and ask the board for their feedback — a little self-evaluation if you will. Ask if they see the need to improve their performance. Ask them if they're ready for change…

I firmly believe that a high-performance board is the #1 most important key to building a successful agency and making a bigger impact.

In our next chapter we'll talk about what an effective board looks like — in action!

CHAPTER 10

What a Great Board *Does*

"To me, ideas are worth nothing unless executed. They are just a multiplier. Execution is worth millions." - Steve Jobs

It's not enough to look (or sound) good on paper. If you want your organization to grow — to have a bigger impact — you must lead your board to *perform* the best that they can.

In our last chapter we covered the 20 characteristics of effective boards. But all of those characteristics are pointless, if your board can't put them into action. So now we'll focus on putting the rubber to the road and getting your board to *be* better.

You may have a great plan and a great collection of people on your team and on the board. Your challenge now is, how to make it all work together successfully? How does this collection of talented individuals with shared values, a shared passion for your agency, and many ideas on how to proceed come together and work collaboratively as a closely-knit team? I am not talking about creating a group of "yes men" but a passionate, dedicated team that will work closely together — notwithstanding occasional differences of opinion — to achieve common goals.

While there are many things your board can do to perform at a higher level, I believe there are 3 critical components that can make a significant difference.

1. Identify the right board chair, create and communicate expectations, and let them truly *lead* your board.

Every successful board is led by an effective board chair. But what makes a board chair effective?

After serving on many boards — several as their board chair — here is my take on what makes a good board chair.

First and foremost, a board chair must be seen as a leader, so the position should go to someone who has displayed leadership competencies while serving on the board. This spot should not be treated as a reward for good behavior, for making large donations, or for being a "good guy". If others see that a person has that certain something true leaders have, things should go smoothly. If not, there could be issues down the line.

Occasionally, the chair will have to make hard decisions or take controversial but appropriate positions on issues. This process is much easier when directors respect the chair and see him or her as having the moral courage to do what is right, not just popular or easy.

An individual lacking in strength of character, or with low self-confidence won't enjoy being a board chair and will likely do a poor job, which can put the agency at risk.

An effective board chair must be assertive when necessary and have command of the board and board meetings. But remember, kindness, grace, and respect will always go a long way towards progress. The rest of the board will appreciate both the strong leadership and empathetic approach.

A board chair should actively manage board meetings. People want to be led and a board is no different. This may be the biggest complaint (and biggest compliment) I hear from others. Most directors work full time jobs, so evening or weekend agency meetings require sacrifice. The least a chair can do is maintain control over the meeting, work to keep it interesting and engaging, and moving along at the quickest pace possible.

A few pointers for effectively managing board meetings (as a board chair).

- Keep discussions on topic and stopping someone who starts getting off point. This means not allowing people to repeat points that were made previously.

- Don't allow directors to revisit recent decisions to a second look. Once decided, that's it!

- Don't hesitate to send an issue to a committee

for study when directors do not have sufficient information to vote.

- Pull aside any director who has become a problem, due to either absenteeism, disrespectful discourse, getting personal, or not being accountable to follow through on commitments.

An effective board chair understands and respects the integrity of the agency organizational structure and processes, leaving management to the CEO/executive director.

An effective board chair maintains an open dialog with the agency's leader. Periodic check-ins are effective at helping to avoid surprises.

As the board chair for one agency I met monthly with the executive director. We would discuss emerging issues, potential problems, new opportunities, and the draft agenda for the next board meeting.

I didn't want any surprises popping up for the board, so whenever something came up that might develop into a problem, the board knew immediately, and we kept it informed until it was resolved.

An effective chair keeps things simple. One way is by using charts and graphs, and asking the agency leader to do the same, whenever possible.

One way to do this is to create "dashboard reports"

to highlight progress on annual goals — financial, programming, etc. If you take time to identify the few key metrics that really matter, and report on them on a regular basis, you will communicate to each person in the organization how you're doing.

2. Delegate details (and heavy lifting) to board sub-committees or tasks forces when necessary and know (or learn) how to manage them effectively.

The one part of board service many directors dislike is attending board or committee meetings, yet effective meetings are a prerequisite to successful agencies. These meetings should be organized, interesting, engaging — and most importantly — as brief as possible to get the job done.

Fortunately, today's trend in the nonprofit world is to have smaller boards and fewer standing committees. Instead, successful boards create ad-hoc committees or task forces to tackle specific issues. This means most directors will probably serve on only one committee (other than board officers).

For example:

Perhaps your organization is looking to move into a larger space. Rather than hand the project off to a standing operations-type committee, an effective board may create a task force to conduct research and report back to the board.

Board committees are where the "heavy lifting" usually takes place for the board. Important or complex issues are sent to be studied and evaluated "off-line" so they can be reviewed carefully without using up board meeting time. Once its work is completed, the committee can present a well-informed report and its thoughtful recommendations to the board on how to proceed.

There are few common standing committees most agencies have, but there can be valid reasons to have others as well. These committees generally remain open throughout the life of the nonprofit, where as an ad-hoc committee or special task force is disbanded once a particular project is complete. Some of the most common standing committees are as follows:

- Governance/Board Development Committee
- Audit/Financial Committee
- Executive Committee (in a few cases)
- Marketing/Fund Development

As a general rule of thumb, there are very few agenda items that should be brought up to the entire board for discussion, on their first mention. This typically wastes time, as most directors are speaking without much knowledge, perspective or context. Instead, these items should be handled by a committee until it is time for the board to make a decision.

I once served on a board that tried to discuss which health insurance program to select for the staff. Can you imagine 17 people discussing insurance options at 9pm? Needless to say, it didn't go well.

Thankfully the board chair formed a task force to assess the options and come back with recommendations at our next meeting. We were able to fully evaluate the programs, the companies involved, and the costs so we could provide our staff with the best value we could find.

An important side-note on committees.

There is usually nothing in the bylaws preventing non-board members from co-serving on committees with board members. This allows you to bring on board candidates or others who have specific and helpful knowledge that will help the committee.

3. Create (and manage) board meetings people actually *want* to attend.

Here are some tips for leading good board meetings.

- Set board meeting dates one year in advance so everyone can block out the time far in advance.
- Send out the meeting agenda and all key supporting documents one week in advance and ask your directors to read everything and be ready to discuss them, vote on them, or make any other decisions required.
- Don't be afraid to insist they come to meetings prepared and ready to discuss issues. If needed, tell them there won't be any time to read the package during the meeting.
- Keep your agendas high level.

Remember, your board of directors has been charged with looking out 3-5 years to help the agency prepare for the future. They also have certain oversight responsibilities. They are smart people with many skills and a great network.

- Use meeting time to pick their brains, seek their input and opinions. Let them brainstorm periodically to learn what emerging trends they see on the horizon for your agency.

- Don't waste the board's time with detailed things that don't matter.

- Your board may not like it, but they may need periodic retraining on important issues.

    Don't avoid the occasional deep-dive into a controversial or complex issue. Keep in mind, they will have forgotten much from their original New Director Orientation and Training so take time to refresh them on parts of it as needed.

- Be sure the board Secretary captures all action items and next step items discussed at the meeting, including who is responsible to take action, and by when.

This will significantly increase the chances that directors will complete all assignments they are given and follow through on any commitments they make. It is entirely appropriate to hold people accountable for what they say they will do. Some directors will be completely reliable but some — and you know who they are — will need a check in every so often by the chair, to ensure everything gets done.

If you really want to bring some life into an upcoming board meeting, or want to get directors thinking in new ways, you might try one of these conversation starters.

- Assume we are an entirely brand-new board and leadership team. We've been brought into this agency overnight and handed the problems and issues the agency currently faces. What are the top 3 things we should do immediately?

- Let's assume we're holding another board meeting 3 years into the future. We're excited because we've been so successful in our mission. Looking back from then, what decisions did we make today, what actions did we take starting today, that set us up for the success we are enjoying 3 years from now?

- If we were creating and starting our agency today — brand new — what skill sets would we want to have on the board? How would the board be composed? How would the organization be set up?

- Pick one of the agency's Core Values and go around the board table and ask each director what that value means to them. What does it look like when you see it happening at the agency?

- Read 2-3 letters (in confidence) from recent clients who used your services and took the time to write a thank you note. As them for their reaction and how those letters might impact the agency's work in the future.

Putting it All Together

We've talked about what a good board member looks like. We've talked about the 20 characteristics vital to building a successful board. We've discussed what a great board looks like in action. You now have a solid idea of what you're shooting for… but as hard as we all might wish we can't just snap our fingers and have a successful board.

My guess? After reading the last few chapters you've currently found yourself in one of two categories. The few extremely lucky leaders that say, "Ok, my board needs a little work, but I can easily see it getting there…" or the side where the rest of us end up… "My board is a mess and I don't even know where to start."

Believe me, I get it. I've been on many boards that fell squarely into category two. There is hope. You've picked up this book. You've read this far. I believe you can make this happen. If you start with just a few areas to focus on, you will start to see change right away.

If it all seems overwhelming — and if you're normal it does — I can offer one suggestion. Start with the 3 Critical Components of what a good board *does*. Get yourself a good board chair, rethink your committees (and *use* them) and start running better board meetings. These three will help to lay the groundwork to make the 20 Characteristics of an Effective Board possible.

In our next chapter we'll talk about the real world that goes on outside of leadership books and what to do when things go wrong…

FROM THE INSIDE OUT

CHAPTER 11

Houston, We Have a Problem
How to Deal with Board Challenges

"We can't solve problems by using the same kind of thinking we used when we created them." --Albert Einstein

We've talked about creating great board members. We've gone over what an incredible board looks like and how it should operate. In theory you have everything you need to build a board to take your agency to the next level. Except for one thing… knowing what to do when it all goes wrong.

When you're dealing with people — in real world situations — things will inevitable spring up to thwart your best laid plans. You'll have that one board member that just wreaks havoc on your organization. You have two years of running less-then-successful board meetings and now you somehow have to get everyone doing something better. Your board chair needs to go. So now what?

I want to take some time in our last chapter about boards to talk about some of the key challenges faced by agencies just like yours, and what you can do to make them better.

First and foremost, I want you to remember — leading nonprofit board members is not always easy. In fact, it may never be a walk in the park. But my hope is to make many of the challenges easier for you, and quicker to deal with and resolve.

Sooner or later, every nonprofit leader has a problem with a board member. How this issue is dealt with separates the successful leaders from the rest of the pack. You may find certain board members are causing unnecessary problems. Yet, you want to maintain peace and retain them as directors. How can you accomplish this? It's easier said than done.

Have you experienced any of these sticky situations in your leadership?

Common Board Challenges

- Personal friends or family members serving on the board no longer add value or become a distraction.

- Your directors want to be nice and not hurt feelings – so they fail to speak truth. They forget their governance role and no longer speak their minds.

- Directors fail to live up to their donation and fund- raising commitments.

- A board member consistently fails to deliver on his/her commitments and obligations as an officer of the agency.

- Directors don't come to meetings prepared or ready to engage. The meeting starts, and everyone is scrambling to read the agenda/meeting packet.
- You'd prefer to not offer a second term to a board member just finishing their initial term.
- A board member consistently rambles in meetings and rarely adds substance to the discussion.
- Long-serving board members believe their opinions are worth more than new directors and become overbearing, bottlenecks, naysayers, or change-resistant.
- Directors take a relaxed approach to their duties.
- Directors get personal and attack a specific person, rather than the issue.
- Directors seem to have a personal agenda around certain topics.

So, what do you do in these situations? How do you handle them?

My experience tells me that too many leaders simply hope the problem goes away, that the offending director somehow "gets" the message, or they hunker down until the offending director's board term is up.

Sometimes I hear excuses like, "Their heart is in the right place because they are doing God's work." or,

"They are helping our vets get re-established." All wonderful causes — definitely worth serving — but not good enough to put up with poor behavior.

In fact, it can be exactly *because* someone is either doing God's work or helping our vets that a leader should feel a higher responsibility to have the very best and most effective board possible. That means you can't ignore tough situations like these.

I believe all the examples above call for a face-to-face, heart-to-heart conversation with the offending director (or the entire board) about the negative effect they are having on the board (and potentially the agency). A poor performing nonprofit board member can keep your team from operating at peak levels.

Many people like hearing facts when an important change is needed.... I know I do. For some directors, sharing hard facts that illuminate the impact of their behavior is enough to get them to change. For others, an appeal to their emotional side will do the same thing.

Regardless of approach taken, you and your board chair know your board's demeanor and culture better than anyone. You should encourage the chair to take the lead in addressing these behavioral problems before they become ingrained habits. Remember, leadership requires having the moral courage to say what needs to be said to those who need to hear it.

When Your Board Falls Short of Expectations

One fairly common frustration I hear from executive directors is that their board is not providing the leadership, guidance, and support the organization needs. This comment is often followed by their admission that they are afraid to bring this problem up with their board for discussion.

I totally get it — this is a tough position to be in. Your "boss" is not providing what you feel you need to lead well but you are a little nervous about how to bring it up in a positive, constructive way.

Here are some approaches you can take to get the conversation started in a safe environment.

- Stick to facts. Can you demonstrate that your agency is not having the impact on your community and a new refocus or back to basics approach may be necessary? I suggest you focus on impact/results, goals, and activities and avoid people issues for now.

- How's your strategic alignment? Can you provide the board with examples of people and programs in your agency that are not all headed in the same direction? Maybe even fighting each other for resources?

- Can you cite clear and compelling examples of the board not delivering on critical previous promises?

- Are the agency's goals consistently missed?

- Is there a lot of confusion or waste surrounding priorities, and how to best use your people, financial and other resources?
- Does your agency experience false start-ups and the existence of orphan projects?
- How long has it been since you developed, updated, or reviewed your progress on your strategic plan?
- Are more than your agency's share of poor decisions being made?
- Are you experiencing higher turnover than normal?

Sometimes if enough of these questions raise concern in the minds of your directors, they will be open to participating in an objective, confidential, board assessment. Assessments offer directors the opportunity to rate a number of key areas of nonprofit and board activity by how important they are AND how well the directors are performing in them.

When Directors Follow Instead of Lead

Another challenge leaders face is having passionate board members who do not lead or seem lost.

Sadly, there are many executive directors who feel their board is failing when in fact, it may not be the fault of the board members at all. The issue can often be a lack of effective board training and not setting clear expectations for your board. Weak and untrained boards cause frustration and can hurt your agency's performance.

It's no secret that effective leadership is important. A good place to start when resolving board issues is to focus on setting clear expectations and investing in board training.

I think sometimes CEO's forget that many directors have never previously served on a board. New directors may actually be trying very hard but they if they were never told what it means to be a director and what that job entails, how can anyone expect them to deliver?

New directors probably have no idea what a director does aside from raising money, participating in events, and the like. Too often, new directors are never really told what their roles and responsibilities are and what is expected of them. They simply have never been trained in these areas.

New directors are rarely briefed on the agency's current issues, problems, and opportunities. Instead, they are expected to just absorb all this on their own.

The solution is to set clear expectations and make sure candidates are briefed even before being voted onto the board. Before a candidate becomes a director, he/she should learn about the issues the board is currently facing. Whether they are financial, staffing, community engagement, growth related, or otherwise. A new director cannot be expected to add value until he/she becomes informed.

Another way to solve this problem is to conduct an effective new director board training program.

Inexperienced directors sit out most discussions, at least early on, and let the older directors carry the load. This means the agency is cheated out of the full board's wisdom. Instead, the board only gets input from a few directors. What a waste of talent.

You can unleash huge amounts of wisdom, energy, and new ideas by ensuring you have an effective director orientation program and conduct periodic board refresher training. With a little planning and extra effort, an executive director and a board chair can provide other directors with a board training program catered specifically to your nonprofit. This helps provide valuable and effective board leadership, translating into dynamic results for your agency's mission.

How to Deal With Difficult Board Members

What do you do when a good board member goes bad? One of the most important tasks you face is to help the board chair and governance committee identify and "vet" new board candidates. You use comprehensive checklists, you interview a wide range of people, you consider what skills/talents our strategic plan requires, you consider your key volunteers/partners. Finally, you create the best panel of candidates you can and invite them to join the board.

So far, so good. The orientation goes well, and each new director is excited to be joining the team. For a while, things go great, and it seems you've landed a high value, hard-working board. But then, something starts to subtly shift.

One or two of your board members starts becoming difficult to work with. There was no single trigger event causing this change, it just starts happening in little ways. The director becomes difficult to please, unreasonable, argumentative, or just no longer wants to work as part of a team.

What happened? Chances are, it wasn't one thing. But no matter how hard we try, no matter how experienced we are at board building, sooner or later nearly every nonprofit leader faces this problem. And it's a tough one.

All executive directors and board chairs want smart, dedicated, creative thinkers serving on their boards—people who will speak truth and can be counted on to always give their best efforts.

We can easily deal with directors who might cause a bit of healthy friction during board discussions as long as they stick to the issues and avoid getting personal or rude. After all, no one should want a room full of *yes people* serving on the board. All one can ask is that it be done in a respectful and professional way. Most of the time, that's exactly what we get, but from time to time a board member may become a problem.

So, what do you do with a problem board member?

First, remember that each director was careful identified and recruited onto the board — to fill a specific need — so they should be treated well and recognized as the asset they are to the agency. They have a critical role to play, and if possible, you still want to tap into their skill-set, talents, or experience.

While often appealing, simply hoping things will improve over time, without taking action, is not a solution. The environment at board meetings will probably just get more negative. Worse yet, avoiding the issue may signal to other directors that this is acceptable behavior, creating more of what you don't want.

Recognize that dealing with this challenge effectively requires the active support and participation of the board chair or governance committee chair — ideally to take the lead. This is not the time for an executive director to go it alone and approach the director in question.

Have a conversation with the board and governance committee chairs to see if they agree that this has become a problem situation. Invite their insight and perspective on the issue and see if they believe it is an overall board challenge, or perhaps only a challenge one-on-one between this board member and you.

Sometimes your leadership and communication style or overall approach may not fit well with each of the directors on the board. In this case you would need to consider modifying your approach — if you want to retain this director — and create a better working relationship, or work towards replacing this individual on the board.

If your board chair and/or governance committee chair feel your style and approach were not causing the problem, and this challenge was more global to the board itself, then it's time to gather facts supporting your concern about the director's behavior and how it has and continues to impede the agency's mission and progress.

Create a plan of how to address these concerns with the director in question. Rehearse the conversation ahead of time to help smooth out the tougher points. I would encourage you to speak with an HR or Organizational Development Professional who can offer specific advice for framing conversations like this. It will need to be handled in a professional, tactful, and non-abrasive manor.

Then meet with the director to discuss the challenge. This meeting should include the board and/or governance committee chair. Keep in mind, the goal of this meeting is to bring about positive change. While it can be tempting to vent frustrations, try to keep emotions out of the conversation and instead stick to the facts at hand.

Remember, all of you should have the same goal in mind — moving the organization forward.

Dealing with board challenges — especially those that involve a specific individual — can be difficult and draining. If you're human — and like many of us — your initial approach may be to delay dealing with a difficult conversation or situation in hopes that it will improve on its own over time. I can tell you from personal experience... this rarely ever happens. A bad board member is like a bad apple. It only takes one to ruin the whole batch.

The key to dealing with difficult people and making tough decisions is to focus on the end game and stick to the facts when possible. Refresh yourself on your vision, mission, and values. Remind yourself that this particular board member is not helping you move forward — and may even be pushing you backwards. They may be creating friction on your board and putting other (good) board members at risk.

Just like keeping a bad employee around, holding onto a bad board member, can reflect poorly on you as a leader. If you are willing to step up and make the tough calls your team (and board) will respect your character as a leader.

PART 4:

LEADING CHANGE

FROM THE INSIDE OUT

CHAPTER 12

Getting Ready for Change

It's not the destination that's difficult, it's the journey.

Almost everyone wants to be somewhere better. But very few can fully embrace the process of *getting* there.

Change. Is. Hard.

Why? Let me let you in on a little secret…

Neuroscience tells us the human brain isn't actually wired to embrace change — it's wired for security. Many people see change not as potentially positive, but instead as a threat to their current survival, safety, and comfort. Even if things aren't great, most people are willing to endure, rather than risk the possibility that the unknown could be worse.

It doesn't really matter if moving to that newer cave creates a bunch more opportunities for building better wheels. Unless there's a bear breathing fire at us in the current cave, our brains say it's best to hold. After all, you never know… the new cave could have a loch ness monster… Besides, who wants to try and convince the other cave dweller to help you move…

In addition, that same science tells us we are *all* creatures of habit, and our brains are to blame for that as well. In an effort to conserve precious resources, our brains create habits — repetitive things that can be done without conscious thought.

Imagine having to stop and remember all the steps involved in brushing your teeth each morning. While a reminder to not drip on your shirt before a big meeting would be helpful, in general we want our brain power available for bigger and better things. This whole "creatures of habit" thing is yet another reason change is difficult.

Remember that time you decided to take a new way home from the office because there was an accident? Even though you knew exactly where you were headed, you probably had to stop and double check a few things on your way, just to make sure. You might have even taken a wrong turn if you weren't paying close attention.

Learning new things, or doing things in new ways, is taxing. It literally requires our brains to work harder. So of course — since we're wired for survival — we will resist change (and effort) whenever possible.

Does that mean there's no hope for change? Not at all. I've seen many agencies (and the people in them) change significantly for the better. You just need to know how to make it happen. It's my goal for this last section of the book, to help you succeed at change.

Recognizing the Need for Change

As a leader, you should be one of the first to recognize the need for change. You are looking both into the future — determining how to position your agency — and at the day-to-day operations, making sure things are on track.

There are a number of things that can tip you off to the need for change.

- Expenses continuously increase
- Program results continuously slip, and critical client needs go unaddressed
- Governmental or funding source changes
- Difficulty in decision-making and priority-setting
- Confusion or disagreement on direction
- Everyone is working hard but results continue to disappoint
- Mission creep has taken the agency down too many unrelated paths so the agency must be refocused
- There has been significant turnover of board or team members and everyone needs to get on the same page.
- The agency has too many priorities or no priorities.
- Team (and board) roles and responsibilities are unclear and people are stepping on each others' toes.

- A lack of accountability on the board or staff.
- Decisions are driven by passion, not strategy

No matter how long your agency has been around, or how successful it's been, there comes a time in every leader's career when he or she recognizes that the tried and true ways of getting things done aren't working very well anymore.

Do any of these situations sound familiar?

- Costs are rising and need to be managed better without cutting core services.
- Significant financial donations that were promised, have fallen apart due to changes in the economy or shifting donor interest.
- Maybe your agency is a huge success and growing but your old processes and procedures are unable handle it.
- Perhaps changes in your community are forcing you to rethink your priorities and internal processes.
- Funders either pull back or ask for additional and more detailed proof of your effectiveness.
- Your clients' challenges and needs have changed so your current programming no longer serves them very well.

There are many signs that an agency needs to think about change.

Regardless of how you got there, you've come to

the point where you realize that staying where you are, operating as you have, is no longer an option. You really don't want to open that "change" can of worms, but in your heart, you know if you don't, your agency's future could be in jeopardy.

So, what do you do?

If change is handled poorly, you may create fear, confusion, and concern about the future viability of your organization. But you know you can't ignore the evidence. Change has to happen, but just what kind of change, how, and when?

Leading change can be like navigating a kayak through the rapids. You know where you're headed but the path keeps changing and the unexpected bumps along the way can take you off course. My goal is to help you prepare yourself as a leader, and your organization, to create positive lasting change.

First and foremost, remember your first responsibility in the change process is not to try and change processes or operations.

This goes back to the creatures of habit. Throwing out all the chips in the house doesn't change the habit of binging snacks and Netflix after a tough day at the office. You'll just end up frustrated, scavenging through the cabinets for something else. If you really want to change the habit, you'll need to look at replacing your nightly binge of mind-numbing entertainment with a walk around the block.

Your primary goal in the change process — and the first thing to work on with your team is changing culture. Before anyone will respond to your call for change, you'll need to change hearts, minds, and attitudes. If you can do that, you're half way there. In fact, if you do it well, your team will even help you identify the changes needed and work to make them a reality. They will appreciate that you notice problems and want to work towards making things better for them.

But before they will embrace change, they need to believe you and understand *what* needs to happen, and *why*. Remember the cave... No one is moving without seeing the bear. And even if they do see the bear, they still need a nice cave painting of the new digs and the wheel factory by the river. Just make sure your cave painting is fire and bear free.

Second on your list of making change happen — be ready to answer many, many questions. Often the same question over and over. Patience, empathy, and understanding will take you far. Keep in mind, people generally like the change once complete, they just hate the process of change and the uncomfortable and *unknown* mess between today and tomorrow.

Remember the fear of the unknown? We don't like it, and it scares our brains, so we'll do something — anything — to make it better. Your team may be inclined to make facts up about the change. Rumors will run wild and people have lofty imaginations so you'll need to be as transparent and consistent as possible, sharing information as best and as fast as you can.

The new cave is bigger, with trees outside. The wheel factory will create 43 new jobs and runs on clean energy. The entire area has been cleared of loch ness monsters — twice.

Try your best to never lie to or mislead your team. Your credibility is at risk and it may be one of the best tools you will have to get everyone through this challenging time together. There will be times you don't have information to share. That's ok. Be upfront and tell them that but let them know you will share information as soon as you have it.

Developing the Case for Change

When you suspect changes are needed, you'll need to gather facts to build your case for change. Your board and team will need some convincing that the status quo is no longer tenable. The data may also tip you off about what kind of change is needed, or to what extent. Do you really *need* a new wheel factory, or do you just need a cave without bears?

Gather as much data as reasonably possible to back up your case that changes are needed. You don't need to have all the answers, just the highlights to prove the agency needs to take a look at itself and fix whatever the challenges are.

Negative trending of expenses, declining program results, or less client successes, are all metrics that may provide the foundation you'll need to convince others of the need for change. Not only will you need the data to convince people of the need, but you'll also need data to convince everyone why their roles, processes, etc. will eventually need to change.

In many cases, facts and data will be enough for people to initially support change. But keep in mind — especially in a nonprofit — people are there because of a passion or concern for a cause. Numbers may be important, but they may not be enough for some of your team members. You will need to become an effective story teller — painting a picture of what could happen.

If one of your key board members hears the stats but doesn't support change, you may need to give a specific example of how services will be reduced, impacting clients. Talk about Mary, with her three children — Danny, Emily, and little Beth — that won't be able to get help anymore. Data may tell a story, but empathy and emotion make it much more vivid.

Measuring your own current results against previous times is a great way to assess trends in your agency. But if there is comparative data available about other agencies, you should try to access it so you can compare your results to the "industry" averages.

Next, you'll need to speak to your directors about what you suspect and provide them with whatever information and data you have. You might even take current trends and project them 3-5 years into the future. This can make your case for change even stronger. Sometimes, people need to see the future not just be told of it so make reasonable projections of where things seem to be headed. Use graphs, charts, and photos if possible, not just numbers. Your case will appear much stronger.

You'll need to figure out the best way to present this information to your board. This can be tough. I would suggest you "pre-sell" the content to your chair, the executive committee, or a few directors you think would look most favorably on your recommendation. Ask them for suggestions on how to "sell" the idea to the others. The most important thing is to create a compelling enough reason for change to secure the support of the board.

Remember, your entire team will be watching you closely — even leaning on you — during the process of change, so you'll want to show visible commitment to the new vision. They will want to see how you are handling change.

You must show you believe in the process and are committed to achieving the new results. They will want to know if you're being totally open, consistent, and honest with them or if you are hiding something. Your demeanor in the office, how you respond and treat others all comes under tighter scrutiny.

Everyone will benefit if you can maintain and communicate a sense of urgency. If you say changes must be made for the good of the agency and those it serves, then to be consistent, those changes need to be identified and implemented as soon as possible.

Once you secure the board's agreement, you're ready for the next phase — planning for change.

CHAPTER 13

Planning for Change
(Creating a Workable Strategic Plan)

If you don't know where you're going, any path will do.

I'll admit it. As a general rule, I don't like to carefully read and follow directions before taking on some project. I'm the person that's had to build a piece of furniture... twice — before it works. And only on the second or third try do I reach for the directions, and that's only because my shortcut didn't work.

Why does it seem there is never enough time to do the work on a project right the first time, but there always seems to be enough time to do it over? Most of the time, I end up wishing I had followed the instructions.

Except for a certain Swedish-based furniture company — yes, I'm talking about you. You will never win. Even though you simplify your instructions to as few words as possible, using mostly pictures of happy or sad stick figures and dozens of sketches of 48 different screws, I *still* won't read them. You will not win my soul in your game... I will defeat you.

Unfortunately bringing about positive change in a nonprofit is a little trickier than building a 73-part desk. And the consequences of having to do it over two or three times can be a lot worse than a wasted weekend...

What you need to bring about change in your organization is a solid set of instructions — sans the happy/sad faced stick people. For an agency, we call this set of instructions a Strategic Plan.

Referenced in the beginning of our leadership journey together — a Strategic Plan lays out the most direct route to your goals. All you have do is follow it (and remain open-minded enough for the occasional small detour). A strategic plan is a high-level overview of the direction an agency will follow to accomplish its mission. The plan identifies several (3-5) high-level objectives where the agency will focus. It also includes SMART goals or targets to be achieved along the way.

Why Strategic Plans are Important

A well-thought out plan will help in several ways.

- They give everyone a common understanding of the purpose, direction, and focus
- They promote unity from the boardroom to the mailroom
- They frame all decisions and focus how the agency uses resources in a specific time and direction
- They outline the fastest and least costly way to

accomplish your goals

- They make it easier to avoid disagreement and to say "no" to some good or even very good ideas that are not relevant to your current mission so you can maintain focus
- They make for clearer:
    - Priority-setting
    - Budgeting
    - Marketing and branding
    - Fundraising
    - Recruiting of directors and team members
    - Organizational structure
- A good strategic plan enables your team members to move quickly and make better and faster decisions by giving them a roadmap to refer to.

With a good plan everyone knows where the agency is headed, and what it considers to be its primary goals, so everyone can focus their efforts on those outcomes. No expensive and wasteful guess work, and no personal-driven "re-lobbying" for pet projects.

Strategic plans are also powerful fundraising tools. Donors are no longer willing to simply write checks and assume the funding will be put to good use. Most donors want relationships. You'll need to capture their imagination by painting a compelling vision of your work and how their support will help make it happen.

Your agency's strategic plan will be one of the most effective tools you have in your leadership toolbox. It should become your best friend. Used appropriately it should help you solve problems, provide direction to your team, and help you make good decisions.

So how do you go about creating a great Strategic Plan, or updating the one you have so it's actually workable? We will tackle that next.

Key Components of a Strategic Plan

An important note to begin with... While all strategic plans have an almost universal set of elements there is no one exact way to create your perfect plan. There are many similar steps leaders take, but the process often becomes organic and takes off in directions no one anticipated. Many agencies use a facilitator to help craft their Strategic Plan. These individuals know when to let the discussion flow and when to bring everyone back to the process.

What we will go over in this book are the universal set of elements for creating a Strategic Plan. Depending on your organization you may have a variety of other items included in your plan. This is perfectly fine, although I would give you one point of caution. When creating your plan try to keep to the high level — the *where, what,* and *why* as it were. Leave the exact *how* for your team to decide when carrying out your plan.

Key Component 1: Vision Statement

A strategic plan begins with a Vision Statement. This is a high level, aspirational statement of what your agency would like to see the future look like. Some say to think big and make it something that may never even happen.

Key Component 2: Mission Statement

A mission statement describes specifically *why* your agency exists. It describes what role your agency will play as you pursue your Vision. Sometime people get confused about the differences between a mission and a vision. The way I keep them straight is by thinking of the vision as an almost unachievable future you want, and the mission statement as what part of the vision you will play.

For example, see the three agency vision statements and their corresponding mission statements below and note the difference between the two.

Example *Vision* Statement 1: Eliminate Hunger in our Community

Example *Mission* Statement 1: To operate a full-service food pantry providing culturally appropriate and nutritious foods to our guests.

Example *Vision* Statement 2: To improve the overall quality of life throughout our community.

Example *Mission* Statement 2: To foster philanthropy and connect donors to the community's greatest needs.

Key Component 3: Values Statement

A values statement lists the behavioral ground rules an agency has agreed to follow. It describes acceptable and desirable behavior and conduct (and conversely unacceptable and undesirable conduct) when anyone is engaged in agency activities.

The values apply to internal and external behaviors, to everyone (whether a part of the agency or not), and to the board. Some agencies will stick with single words, some will use phrases or sentences to help further define those words. There is no right or wrong way, as long as you are clear on the values and can communicate them to everyone involved in your organization.

Here are a few common examples of Values words:

- Faith
- Integrity
- Respect
- Collaboration
- Teamwork

You can find many other examples of Values words, with a quick search online.

Here are a few examples of Values Statements:

- We value families and communities, their inherent strengths, their ability to grow, be resilient and find solutions to challenges.
- We value staff professionalism, ethical service

delivery and programs that reflect our compassion for people.

- We believe in effectively managing the contributions of our donors and funders through maintaining sound fiscal policies while striving for excellence.

- We value expeditious decision-making and informed risk taking in pursuit of our mission and strategies.

Key Component 4: Strategic Priorities

These are the high level themes the agency has decided to pursue to achieve its mission. They are intended to be achieved over the short-mid-term, say 2-3 years, though some agencies look out at a 3 to 5-year window. I prefer 3 years max since things can change so quickly and new unanticipated trends and issues pop up frequently.

This is where the agency's focus of attention and emphasis should be placed. Any ideas that don't fit under one or more of your strategic priorities should be tabled until a new plan is developed.

This limited focus on only a few ideas is how you channel energy and direction onto your very top priorities and thereby actually get them done!

A word of caution, though. It is very tempting to take on too much at one time. Some agencies take on too many priorities and get very little done. You are much better off to limit your priorities to 3-5, maximum. Any more than 5 and you will likely have too much going on at one time.

Remember, you'll need to continue operating your agency while trying to work on these priorities. You can risk burning out your team by expecting more than what is reasonable.

Here are some examples of strategic priorities an agency might have created:

- Develop local partnerships to raise awareness about joblessness and to bring employers into the community.
- Invest in the professional development of our leadership team, key staff and volunteer leaders to prepare them for anticipated growth.
- Develop and conduct director orientation and training programs to equip them to serve effectively in those capacities

Key Component 5: Goals

These are the very specific steps to be taken to achieve your strategic priorities. The better crafted they are, the easier it will be for others to follow and accomplish.

The best way I've found to ensure goals are crafted well, is to follow the SMART Goals Model. SMART goals are Specific, Measurable, Achievable, Relevant, and Time bound. Let's look at these in detail.

Specific — What exactly is to be done? Can everyone understand it? Will each of them recognize it they achieve progress? Will they know when it's done? They should answer who, what, when, where, and how.

Measurable — How can you monitor and assess progress on the goal? How will you know when the goal has been accomplished? What meaningful things can be measured to give you a true picture of progress?

Achievable — Goals should be achievable but should also include an element of stretch. What is realistically achievable, under the circumstances? I could set a goal to play professional baseball, but it's probably not going happen in my lifetime, so I may want to modify that goal.

Relevant — Goals should be relevant to your situation and in alignment with one or more of the strategic priorities. They should have significance and matter. If not, they shouldn't be there. If one of your strategic priorities is to reduce your overall expenditures by 25%, creating a goal of moving into a new space twice the size of your current space, may not be relevant.

Time bound — Goals should have a specific completion date, otherwise they are just wishes. I want to run a marathon is nice dream. I want to run a marathon this year (while a bit ludicrous for me) would be an example of a Time bound goal.

Key Component 6: Metrics

What you measure matters, and what you measure gets improved. The things you measure get better because it helps direct everyone's attention and focus.

Metrics work best — and will help pull you toward your goals — when you measure the right things.

At one time, nonprofit donors wanted know numbers — the number of people who came to your agency, the number of people you housed, or fed. Now, they want to know how many people became independent under your agency, how many jobs you found, how long it takes for a client to become successful by following your programs, and has that time been improving.

Key Component 7: Accountabilities

Accountabilities: Each strategic priority and each goal needs a home — a person or a team that is responsible to achieve it. They should be required to provide progress reports periodically to ensure acceptable progress is being made. I recommend these be reviewed at each team or board meeting to keep the momentum moving forward and to identify any significant issues.

Other Items

Some strategic plans may include additional detailed elements, like the history of the agency, emerging trends, internal and external scans, staffing comments, etc., but they are not critical to having your own plan. My goal is to help you create a simple, easy-to-understand, workable plan. A beautiful 150-page binder might look great on a shelf, but it's not ideal for getting things done.

Now that you know what should be in your Strategic Plan, I'd like to end by sharing a few lessons I've learned the hard way. Hopefully these suggestions will make your planning process easier and create a better, more workable plan.

Who should participate in the planning process?

I suggest board and key staff be a part of your planning team. The board understands where the agency is headed and owns the mission, while your staff understands the ins and outs of making it all happen. The board will protect the mission, ensure sustainability, and keep everyone focused on the future. Key staff understand how things get done and can add insight into what is possible.

Some agencies like to have a closed plan next session. I'm in favor of bringing in subject matter experts whenever possible.

While preparing for strategic planning session for a social service agency where I served as board chair, we agreed to bring in an outsider to help provide insight. This person had a commanding knowledge of the demographics in our community and helped us identify emerging trends so we could prepare to meet the new needs of our clients in the future. She was a tremendous help in that she brought a sense of reality, fact, and validation of the direction we were headed.

Who owns the plan and the process and who is responsible to execute the plan?

The executive director is the chief caretaker of the agency and therefore is responsible to make the strategic plan happen. While everyone owns their piece of the plan it's up to the executive director to coordinate all the moving parts and ensure that the plan is being followed.

To help implement the plan and see that it proceeds in a orderly and continuous direction, leaders can develop an implementation or execution plan, which is a detailed breakdown of the steps necessary to accomplish the goals created. While some people can work well from a high-level strategy most of us need a detailed set of steps to follow to carry out a comprehensive strategic plan. Desks get built much faster if you actually do what the stick people tell you to do…

Who should facilitate the planning process?

It's probably best that neither the executive director or a member of the board serve as the facilitator. Since the facilitator roll requires attention to many different areas at once the facilitator is usually unable to actively contribute to the discussion.

The best facilitator is someone who can remain completely neutral so no one can question whether he or she has a hidden agenda. Their job is to serve as the unbiased third party. Their purpose is to help the participants draw the best out of themselves, moderate discussions and disagreements, and to keep them on point and professional. The best facilitator is one who can remain dispassionate and draw out your very best thinking, seeking the best possible outcome for your agency.

How should an agency prepare for a planning session?

First, collect as much data as you can on the areas that are important to your agency and drive results, and then share it with those will be participating. The data should include both internal and external information. Some of the data you might want to include — revenue and its varying sources, client growth and their changing needs, donor trends, financial results, demographic trends, your programming results (costs vs benefits, inputs, outputs, results, impact, etc.)

Whatever areas you can measure should be considered. Since you are there to make important decisions, it is critical that everyone have the same information and that it be as accurate as possible.

Let everyone know in advance that you intend to deal with and base the new plan on facts, not opinions. Some people have great oratory skills and can build compelling arguments to support their opinions. Opinions without facts should be used only sparingly when planning out your next 2-3 years' priorities. While they have an important place in the planning session they should always be clearly labeled so as not to confuse anyone.

Bringing it all Together

Hopefully you have a solid understanding of why a Strategic Plan is important, what goes into making it, and how to create a straightforward simple version your team can actually do.

If you're starting from scratch, I know it can be daunting. The key is to focus on the 7 key elements. It can be easy to fall into the trap of adding things, but if you want to see results on your plan, remember *less is more*.

Change is hard. Changing people — hearts, minds, and attitudes, is even more difficult. Your job is to create a compelling vision of how things could be different and communicate this vision to your team — board, employees, and volunteers. You must become a champion for change.

Remember, nearly everyone *wants* to be in a better place, they just struggle with how to get there. Change almost always elicits fear and hesitance, or at best discomfort. Your role in this change process is to make a case for change, lead your team through the difficult interim, remind them of the forward progress you're making, and continue to paint a picture of the new destination.

CHAPTER 14

Planning for Potholes & Detours
(Why Some Strategic Plans Don't Work)

If you haven't hit any obstacles, you're probably not moving.

I wish I could tell you it's all going to go perfectly. Pitch your idea, create your plan, go nuts. But the reality is, something — perhaps many things — will inevitably go wrong. My goal is to give you as much help as possible to help you succeed in this adventure, we call change. So instead of pretending everything will be fine, let's take a few minutes to think about the potential challenges now, in hopes of preventing them.

In their bestselling book *Switch: How to Change Things when Change is Hard,* authors Dan Chip Heath said, "Ambiguity is the enemy. Any successful change requires a translation of ambiguous goals into concrete behaviors."

I said it earlier in a few less words. People are afraid of the unknown. They like the idea of heading somewhere new, but that icky-sticky process in the middle? That's a hard sell, and even harder to keep going once started.

Your team may develop the absolute best strategic plan possible for your agency. It may cover all the key issues you needed to address and may be written in a captivating, motivational style.

But it's possible it will still fall flat when you try to make it work. As you work on making your new plan a reality, remember, you as the leader own the responsibility to effectively communicate what is happening and why, throughout the process, even beyond when it's "done." With this in mind, let's look at some of the biggest reasons strategic plans fail.

- Poor or inadequate communication is one of the biggest reasons strategic plans fail. People simply may not understand the strategy at first. The lofty and flowery language often used in a plan can sometimes puzzle those who did not participate in the planning process. "They just don't get it".

- The people involved don't see where they fit. Your staff and volunteers do not see how their current roles fit into the new strategy. Unless they see how their job contributes to the new plan, they will be reluctant to buy into it. At the same time, they may begin to think their role is to be eliminated and they will be let go. Both of these can be a hit for morale and delay getting the plan implemented.

- Your leaders play an important role in implementing the new plan and keeping it from failing. When they fail to reinforce or explain it (sometimes re-explaining it if necessary) staff gets confused and wonders if the new plan is real going to happen or perhaps that was just a nice team exercise? Your job is to make sure *everyone* in a leadership role in your organization understands the plan and is helping to make it a reality.

- Your leaders can easily cause the plan to fail by undercutting it when they do not reinforce and implement the changes that are now required. If your leaders continue to work, seemingly ignoring the new strategy, they send a destructive message that change is not really going to happen.

- Poor communication can wreak havoc on the new strategy in other ways, too. If there is no compelling reason given from the start — showing how important the new plan is — people won't buy in.

    The leader has to explain in clear and easy to understand language why it is no longer feasible for the agency to stay as it is or work as it has been working. If the team can understand (and fully embrace) the reason change is necessary, it increases the chances that they will accept it, support it, and make that change a reality.

- Keeping everything a deep, dark secret will cause problems. Try to share whatever you can ahead of any changes so the team has time to think it all through, even before they know what changes are coming.

- When introducing major change, a leader has to

use clear, simple language and the message needs to be consistent. If there are three main reasons for the change, then those three reasons must be referenced continuously throughout the process. I suggest you use the same language each time, too.

It is critical your team trusts you as the leader. By using clear language, explaining what is happening and why, and consistently sticking with those key points, you will help others come to grips with the changes.

As an example, if you tell your team the three biggest reasons you need change are: overwhelming client need, drastic funding reductions, and overworked team members leading to burnout, you need to stick with these. One month into your new plan you can't switch and tell them the reason you need change is because you need a new space and want to start offering new services. Consistency is key.

- Using unclear or "cute" words and phrases will turn off your team and they might become fearful. This can be another way to kill off the plan before it even gets started. Fear usually paralyzes people. While you cannot eliminate all fear, you can try your best to minimize it. If your team acts out of fear, they will inadvertently undercut your change effort. Stay close to your team and periodically check in to see how they are doing with the changes and unknowns.

- Your obligation to communicate well continues during the change process period. While the changes are being implemented, continually remind everyone why the changes are necessary and why the agency really had no option. During this challenging and sometime fearful time, people can forget the reasons. They may resist change and undercut your efforts if you cannot speak to their hearts and minds.

At one point in my past I had the opportunity to lead a significant operational change for what had previously been a successful company. I found that simply walking around the building and talking to as many people as I could helped me assess how well the changes were being understood and accepted.

My one-on-one chats also helped me pick up the general "feel" of the team as a whole. I balanced my informally obtained information against what I was told by others regarding how things were going. This helped me know when we needed a team meeting and what topics needed further clarification.

- Strategic plans can hit serious road blocks if no one "owns" the plan. The leader must be the plan champion and ensure it is being followed. When unanticipated problems arise, the leader must be ready to step in and fix them.

  Whenever the leadership team gets together, the number one item on the agenda must be the status of implementing the new plan and any changes that are required. While a lot of the detailed work can and should be delegated to others, the leader owns the strategic plan and its implementation. Period.

- Another way the process of change can stall, is when the interim progress (successes) aren't celebrated and shared with others. You can overcome this challenge easily by simply recognizing a person or department that is making progress. Choose a time during a meeting to recognize success publicly, or even host a small party for the organization. Reward the behaviors that help, and you will see more.

- One of the easiest ways for leaders to kill the prospects of adopting a new plan is by not making the hard choices that always come with a new plan. People know what decisions need to be made and they will watch to see if you actually do it. Failing to make those tough calls tells others that you are not really serious about the new plan.

- Does your new plan require you to let someone go? Then do it and do it now. Does it require you to cut some services to clients? Do it, as quickly as you can. Don't hesitate or your team will see it as you back-pedaling on the plan. If you're not embracing the "suck of change" your team won't either. They may even question your dedication to the new vision.

- There are times — even when everyone is supportive of the new plan and its needed changes — the implementation can still fail or be severely weakened. Remember, while all the changes are being made, your agency has its day to day work to do. People need to be served, the operations must continue, etc. It is very easy to let the business of the day-to-day responsibilities take over one's workday.

- When this happens, you have two options. Option one is to look at all the things you're doing and see what you can eliminate or do differently, to free up time for the new plan. Option two is to identify little things you can do to make your plan move forward and set aside a minimum of 1-2 hours per day to work on those things. Even incremental progress, made consistently, will eventually get things going in the direction you want.

- As sure as gravity, unanticipated problems will arise during plan implementation. Those must be addressed quickly and head on. Letting them get in the way and slow down progress sends a bad message to others.

- Most threats to successfully implementing change will surface out in front for everyone to see. However, sometimes people will resist what you are trying to do, even potentially working to sabotage your efforts. How should you handle that?

Let me offer a few suggestions I was able to use when I was leading change. The key to making this work is to have respectful yet direct conversations with any/all individuals involved.

   - I asked them about their concerns and tried to clarify any misunderstandings or inaccuracies.

   - I reminded them of the exhaustive and

inclusive process we undertook that led to the changes being made, and that a wide variety of voices were heard.

- I also reminded them that both internal and external environmental reviews were completed so we could gather as much factual data as possible before making any decisions.

- I reminded them of the benefits of the changes and used the data we had found when appropriate.

- I let them know that each person would ultimately have to decide for themselves if they could support/get behind the changes, or if they would decide it wasn't a fit and would transition away from the company.

While this may come across sounding a bit harsh, it's important to remember the significant investment the agency has made in pushing forward change. Even though I personally didn't even like all the changes we were making, I knew they were required. It was important to have everyone on the team moving forward in the right direction.

This process of leading change is never easy. I get it. I've been there. Your best laid plans will go wrong. Roadblocks will appear on a perfectly smooth road. Potholes will surface just as you were picking up speed. There will even be times you want to give up and go back to the way things were. After all, "The hell you know has got to be better than the hell you don't…" It's easy to think this way when you're in the middle. But I encourage you to keep trying.

Continue to talk about your vision and the new destination with your leaders and entire team. Celebrate your forward progress and successes no matter how small. Show your team (and yourself) that you're gaining traction.

Remind yourself of where you want to go and why. And sometimes, when things get really tough, walk away for a minute, get perspective, and come back. The most important part of making change happen, is the mindset of the leader. If you lead well — even though a swamp — they will follow.

FROM THE INSIDE OUT

CHAPTER 15

Making It All Work
(What You Can Do So Your Plan Succeeds)

Planning is Great, but Execution Wins the Game.

You've made your case for change. Your board bought in. You created your plan. You sold your team on it. Somehow against all the odds you succeeded. You have your whole team — minus a couple mumbling naysayers in the corner — behind your vision for change. You've read through all the things that can cause issues with implementing your plan. You're ready to go!

So, what can you do to make sure your plan succeeds?

I'd like to share a few ideas from change expert and Harvard Business School professor John Kotter. In his e-book *The Eight Step Process for Leading Change,* Kotter outlines eight critical steps to take, to make change actually work.

1. Create a sense of urgency.

When implementing a new plan, there has to be a certain amount of selling involved. It helps tremendously when the whole agency gets excited about the changes and can get behind the efforts to make it happen—now.

Along with the excitement, Kotter suggests you underscore why this has to be done *now* and cannot be put off. If the plans are so critical to future success, you can't really afford to take a slow and steady approach to change.

2. Form a powerful coalition.

Convince key people that change is necessary and bring them along to lead it. You can't do this on your own. Certain members of your team can take on the responsibility of managing the changes through the agency. Don't go it alone.

3. Create a vision for change.

People want to *see* a new destination. They want to imagine the future and what it could be like. Your job as a leader is to paint a vivid vision, and then *lead* your team where they want to go.

4. Communicate the Vision.

We talked about it earlier, but this can't be overstated. It isn't enough for *you* to see the vision. Your team needs to see it, touch it, feel it. Talk about your vision — over and over again. Answer questions. Address concerns. Provide clarity. Talk about ways you can get there and why you want to go. During change you cannot over communicate.

5. Remove obstacles.

Take action quickly to remove barriers, whether human or otherwise. Others will be watching to see how you tackle obstacles so if you take a laid-back approach to addressing them, people may take that as an indication that the changes are not all that real important.

6. Create short-term wins.

Forward movement in a new direction will fuel motivation, no matter how small the steps are. Identify some small wins your team can easily see. Celebrate the wins, no matter how insignificant they may seem. Success creates more success.

7. Build on the change.

Real change runs deep and takes a long time so as your plan and changes are implemented look for ways to use them frequently and as foundations for your next steps. Build on what you create and embed it into the fiber of your agency.

8. Anchor the changes in your agency culture.

The values and key factors behind your vision should show up in your day-to-day work. Make continuous effort to ensure that the changes are impacting every action of your agency. Each person has to step up and be the change the plan requires.

Lessons I Learned the Hard Way

Change. Is. Hard. Just wanted to make sure you didn't forget that. I've been through it several times myself. I hope I can make it a little easier for you. Here's a few things I learned the hard way, so hopefully you won't have to…

Once the new plan has been approved— and perhaps even before— it's a good idea to think about its implications.

Parts of the new plan will probably require changes to important areas of your agency. Organizational structure and management may need to change. Some individuals with new and different skills will need to be recruited and hired. Budget priorities may be impacted. Some services or programs may no longer be offered, and new ones may take their place.

The agency's marketing, communications, and outreach practices may undergo changes. They will be needed to explain what is happening at your agency. Strong communication is critical. Just as your team will fill in the unknown with fabricated facts, outsiders will do the same if they can't easily understand what is happening and why.

Management by walking around (MBWA) is a powerful tool you can use to stay close to your team and learn what's on their mind. There is powerful information to be gained to help usher in the changes.

Be sure to reinforce the new plan through your performance reviews, company messaging, website, posters, social media, etc. Everything should align with your new plan — including agency values.

One way to sell the new vision and strategic plan to others is to describe your envisioned reality of the future. Do it clearly, excitedly, and in detail, so everyone can see how great it is. Describe where the agency is today, all the shortcomings, and all that is missing. Then outline the steps to get to your envisioned, new reality. This way, people can begin to connect what is happening now with the future.

Establish a set of metrics everyone can understand to measure progress. Break them down by department, if possible.

Be careful of what you delegate to others. There are certain mission critical parts of making change that only the leader can do. Don't assume others can do this the way you can.

Learn to say no. I hated saying no but once in a while you may be called upon to help the agency stay pointed at its new north star. Mission creep and continuing to use old ways and practices may be tempting but they can undercut you change efforts.

Post your top 3-5 new strategic objectives all over the building, if possible. Can you hang some posters in your building? Let everyone be reminded of what is happening, where you are going, and why. This keeps them focused on the future and not looking backward.

Use your plan as a recruiting guide as you seek out

new hires for staff and new director candidates for your board. Find people who will get excited about your strategy and help make it happen.

Use your new plan to assess how aligned your agency is. Is the organization set up to maximize opportunities to achieve the plan? Does the budget reflect the new priorities? How about staffing, is it in line with the new plan in mind? Marketing, messaging, and programs: do they all reflect the new agency direction? If not, you've got some work to do.

One of the best ways to keep everyone focused on the new plan is to highlight key elements on all agendas (board and team meetings, public presentations, etc.). That way, it stays top of mind for everyone during the process.

Plan out something that can lead to quick wins which can demonstrate how well things are working with the new plan. This helps create momentum and excitement and helps others get on board quicker, especially those that may be holding the team back.

Remember, this process isn't *supposed* to be easy. Change is one of the hardest things you'll do as a leader. But it is essential if you want to take your organization from where it is, to where you believe it can go. If you have a good plan, buy in from your leadership team, and support from your employees, you *can* make this happen. It won't be easy, but in the end it *will* be worth it.

CHAPTER 16

The End is Never Really Near…
Leadership is a Journey, Not a Destination

The greatest leader is not necessarily the one who does the greatest things. He is the one that gets the people to do the greatest things."
– Ronald Reagan

You've made it! You've reached the end of the book. You've learned about leading yourself, your team, your board, and leading change.

In part one we talked about the importance of understanding and developing yourself as a leader first. If you're not even sure where *you*'re going, it will be very difficult to get anyone to follow. If you didn't take time to work through the first few chapters I invite you to revisit them now to fully understand yourself as a leader. If we want to make a compelling case for change, it starts with us. Want to get your team on board for a change? Let them see you change. If you get to a better place your team will want to be there too.

To effectively lead yourself you must know who you are, understand your strengths and weaknesses, and embrace the characteristics of great leadership.

You must clearly understand the unique role only you can play in the organization and how to align all of your activities around the areas of responsibility only you can do. If you can make this shift happen, you will see dramatic results all around. I know it's not easy, but I promise it's worth it.

In part two we talked about the role you play in effectively leading your team — both your employees and volunteers. Nonprofits can look very different. Your organization may have 10 employees or 100. You might have 5 volunteers or 500. But no matter what your team looks like, we can still learn from the best leaders to develop our teams for greatness. We can learn how to inspire from the heart, make difficult decisions, and earn the respect of those we have the privilege to lead.

In part three we talked about one of the most critical elements to creating an organization designed for impact — successfully leading your board. I can't emphasize enough the importance of having a well-trained and fully engaged board. You have a team of leaders ready and waiting to set direction, support the organization, and champion your mission.

We learned about their role in the organization and how to clarify expectations. We discussed what a great board director looks like, and how you can create them in your agency. We talked about building a strong, cohesive team of board members, and what your board should be *doing*. We ended our section on boards with an important piece — learning what to do when things go wrong.

The final part of our journey was learning how to lead for change. What to do to prepare those yourself and those around you to embrace a new vision and strategy. We talked about how to get your team and directors on board. We talked about the importance of communication and selling your vision. We talked about building your plan. We touched on what to do when things go wrong while implementing your plan, and we wrapped up with advise on how to bring it all together and make it actually work.

We've covered what I believe are the four most critical elements needed to make a bigger impact. My hope is that you have a better idea of how to get your organization from where you are, to where you want to go. My hope is that you have already started to further develop yourself as a leader.

My hope is that you have implemented just a few of the suggestions in this book and are already seeing changes in your team, board, or both. But most importantly my hope is that you now have a plan to bring about change, and the most important element — the belief in yourself as a leader to make that change a reality.

I know you can do it. I believe it because you picked up this book and made it through to the end. That tells me you're serious about it. That tells me you *can and will* make change happen.

Remember, leadership — great leadership — is a journey, not a destination. If you focus on the elements on this book, and work through it in incremental pieces, I know you will make incredible progress. You will change as a leader and those around you will notice it. But you will never really be done.

If you pause every so often and look back on how far you've come... look back on who you used to be, how you would have handled challenges before... what you were capable of before, and what you can do now, you will see how far you've come, and can celebrate the success of your journey.

Leadership begins from the inside out. Change starts with you. If you want your organization to have a bigger impact, you need to start with yourself, develop your team, build your board, and finally lead change.

It's not easy... not by a long shot... but I promise you, it *will* be worth it. You can take your agency, team, and board to exactly where you want them to go, if you focus on leading where it matters most.

EPILOGUE

What to Do When You're Stuck

You've read the book. You've answered the questions. You've paused and reflected on your organization. You've worked through the chapters. You've made changes with your team. You've implemented many of the suggestions I've provided. You built (or revised) your strategic plan. Everyone is on a new course of action, everyone is embracing change, things are just humming. You're happy. Your team is happy. Your board is happy. Donations are rolling in. Your organization is thriving. Your job as a leader has become a piece of cake. You're making a huge impact in your community. Things are running so well you're thinking of expanding to offer more services.

Except… wait… none of that's true… or maybe a little is true, but not nearly as much as you had wanted. You're overwhelmed, you're frustrated, and you might even be feeling a little hopeless at the slow speed of change. Maybe you've read this book and now you're not even sure where to start.

Please. Don't. Give. Up.

You have one of the best and most difficult roles there is. You are a leader. Leading people. And because you're dealing with people, you're struggling. People are…. challenging. In fact, they can be downright impossible at times…

People are resistant to change, wary of new ideas, and set in their ways. They like what was and is and are terrified of the unknown. People have personal agendas and their own ideas. They want to follow but only if you can guarantee them it will all be ok, there won't be any potholes that will hurt too much, no snakes will jump out, and the road will be smooth.

But change doesn't work that way. I love the quote, "What got you here, won't get you there." There is a chasm of "ick" in between where you (and your organization) are now and where you want to be. But the good news? If you have a chasm of ick, then you have a vision of where you want to go. And if you have that, I can help you get there. Even if you don't have a vision yet, I can help you create one.

If you want to make a bigger impact with your organization, and many of the elements in this book resonated with you, I can make a new reality possible for you. I can help you develop as a leader, build a stronger team, develop your board, and bring about positive change.

I've helped many leaders just like you get to a better place. If you're stuck, frustrated, or just overwhelmed, please reach out. I'd love to talk to you more about your agency and pursuit of leadership.

For more information to help develop your leadership, and free resources to lead your nonprofit, please visit my website:

www.TomOkarma.com

ABOUT THE AUTHOR

Tom Okarma is a top-rated nonprofit leadership author, keynote speaker and consultant in strategic planning, board development, and board governance. His devotion to helping nonprofits, combined with over 30+ years of business experience, make him a dramatic force for change, helping nonprofits increase their impact.

Tom has spent the last decade serving and leading on numerous nonprofit boards. He's been there, done that, and learned critical lessons about effective leadership and board development. He is a popular speaker at nonprofit events and frequently shares his thoughts on governance, board development, and leadership on his website and through other organizations online.

Tom is an approachable catalyst for senior leaders and provides senior staff members, stakeholders and boards with an understanding and discerning ear. He has worked with and advised many top nonprofit organizations including Providence International, TMCI International, Bright Hope, Next Level Foundation, People's Resource Center, The Barnabas Group, Christian Leadership Alliance, among many others.

Made in the USA
Columbia, SC
10 August 2019